The Learning Machine

A Hard Look at Toronto Schools

Loren Jay Lind

Anansi/Toronto

MINISTRY OF EDUCATION, ONTARIO
COMMUNICATION SERVICES BRANCH
13TH FLOOR, MOWAT BLOCK
TORONTO, ONTARIO M7A 1L3

Copyright © Loren Jay Lind 1974

Published with the assistance of the Canada Council and Ontario Arts Council

Design: Lynn Campbell
Photo: Susan Gaby

Typesetting by Swift-o-Type
Printed in Canada by The Hunter Rose Company

ISBN: Paper 0-88784-646-7 / Cloth 0-88784-743-9
Library of Congress Card Number: 74-84397

1 2 3 4   74 75 76 77

House of Anansi Press Limited
35 Britain Street
Toronto, Canada

🕷 *The important name in Canadian publishing*

For the memory of my mother, Salome, who wanted my initials to be the same as those of my grandfather, Lafayette Johnston.

Preface

In this book I have described the school system in selective detail, attempting to be incisive, though fair, rather than comprehensive in my general approach. Where I skipped over areas, I can plead only the limits of time and space and my own judgment. I focused on the public system of the City of Toronto, not dealing with the suburbs nor the Catholic separate system, and dealing only briefly with the Metro Toronto School Board.

My inquiry began in the classroom, and went from there into the government of schooling. The political structure delimits and influences what happens in the classroom to such an extent that one cannot fault the teachers, except as they resist getting together with parents to change the system. Two teachers at Duke of York Public School wrote an angry response to Chapter 1, which was published in *This Magazine* in slightly abbreviated form. They said it ignored the repressive conditions in which teachers have to work, and failed to point out the means for fighting back. I will have to leave that mainly to the teachers, but I certainly don't believe the schools' salvation lies in simply getting more "exceptional teachers" into the system. It lies in changing the system so that schooling is a function of democracy, rather than system-bound bureaucracy. I do not attempt here a larger analysis of the ties between the capitalist system and the schools. I will leave that to other writers in the hope that this book will inspire a lot of curiosity about it.

It took a lot of help from my friends. I am especially

grateful to Dan McDonald for his honesty and support as I worked through the first drafts, and to Don Evans for his fine critiques of some of the final chapters. George Martell gave me a sense of the broad picture and some help with organization. And Jane, my wife, was a true friend and source of strength throughout. I want to thank James Polk, too, for his judicious editing which made the message all the more my own.

TABLE OF CONTENTS:

1 **Introduction**

5 **Chapter 1: Two Schools.** In which I visit Dundas Street School in the inner city, and John Ross Robertson School in North Toronto, and show how the routines and disciplines put across the system's message.

26 **Chapter 2: The Rise of New Canadianism.** An essay on the way immigrant children are taken into the school system with little thought for their native tongues, and are rather harshly Canadianized.

56 **Chapter 3: A High School Episode.** The pernicious method of streaming children in Toronto gives the poor and disabled every facility, but leaves them poor and disabled.

75 **Chapter 4: A Last Resort.** This is about special education, the decade's fastest growing field of schooling, which has often ended up creating problem children by the very process of isolating and "treating" them.

93 **Chapter 5: On Having to Read.** A description of the reading mania, and a few observations on why the poor seem to be turned off reading at an early age, and how a child's native powers can be diminished by schooling.

114 **Chapter 6: Doing It at School.** A chapter on sex education, which prepares the setting by breaking down the harsh rigidities of high school, and what this says about the rest of the high school system.

133 **Chapter 7: What It Costs.** An analysis of the fiscal crisis. In which the province is seen to undercut local democracy by making it "easier" for taxpayers.

160 **Chapter 8: The School Bureaucracy.** A look at the hassle between trustees and their professionals, in which secrecy plays a unique role. Who controls education? The Cabinet and the civil service.

180 **Chapter 9: The Coming of SEF.** SEF is the Study of Educational Facilities, a $40,000,000 school building project, through which 32 pre-fab facilities have been put up. A technocrat's paradise, a child's ho-hum.

197 **Chapter 10: The Davis Imperative.** This is to show how central control has moved in on local school boards in Ontario, making them subservient to the greater technocratic aims of the Province, in the name of efficiency and equal opportunity.

216 **Chapter 11: A Learning Community.** Reform must happen in the inner world and outer world at the same time, and the last best chance for it to happen is in the local neighborhood.

Introduction

The prime value in Loren Lind's work in writing this book is that he deals with education at a quite specific and concrete level. Indeed, the quantity of specific and factual material is at times almost overwhelming, and yet it is the stuff out of which educational thinking must be generated. The beauty of this book is its humanity — it never loses sight of the fact that all that matters in education is what happens to the child, what happens to children. No doubt there are other, further facts; no doubt there are other, further interpretations. But Loren Lind has devotedly and systematically interpreted what his keen and searching reporter's eye has observed in the light of what it means for the individual and social growth of your child and mine. Thus, you will not find barren arguments about educational theory, no purple passages of philosophical platitudes, but some simple and profound observations on what actually happens to children, and on some courageous attempts to change.

It would be hard to ignore or mistake the strength of parental feelings — indeed the strength of feelings that we all have — when we begin to deal with educational issues. I have seen groups of parents almost at each other's throats over what on the face of it seem simple academic or administrative affairs. Whether this or that social studies syllabus or text-book should be adopted, whether the bus route should go this way or that — these, and similar issues, can turn neighbors into mortal enemies.

The emotional intensity usually, but not always, shows

itself in various forms of aggression. People fight over issues — parent against parent, parent against teacher, teacher against child, and child against parent. Sometimes, rather than attacking a problem, we find ourselves in full flight away from a real difficulty which should command our attention. Anything rather than face the complex reality of our situation — remove it or remove ourselves, destroy or be overwhelmed, fight or flight. These seem to be the more public expressions of emotions in education today.

There was a time in which we all, as parents, teachers and students, derived great emotional satisfaction from the acceptance of the social and educational system, from a belief in its inherent rightness, and from the assumption that it could be depended upon. Those of us who have sat through weary meetings in which a speech or a lecture has been carefully and boringly read to us may have experienced frustration over the fact that nothing happened, but we have misinterpreted the event. The audience may well have derived great satisfaction from the feeling of dependence — the emotional intensity is great and, in a certain sense, fulfilling. It does not lead to change or to development, but neither does the aggressive display of educational warriors. The passive and impassive audience is enjoying the fact that it needs to do nothing.

Nevertheless, parents have a high level of free-floating anxiety with regard to their children — which is scarcely surprising — and this anxiety is, as it were, available to become connected with specific problems or issues as they arise. And so we see the total anxiety about raising our children properly concentrated on whether or not they should have an open-space school, on whether or not they should learn to read through the Initial Teaching Alphabet, or whatever. A rational or detached view would never suppose that educational salvation or damnation would follow a decision about either matter . . . indeed, both suggestions

Introduction

(with all their positive and negative aspects) may be curiously irrelevant to the raising of children. They may not make any real difference. Why, then, do we argue so much about them and about similar issues? Perhaps it is *because* they do not make any difference. The educational world throws up problems for free-floating anxiety to latch onto, while the real work of education goes relentlessly on.

Traditionally, the school has been built on an assumption of a well-ordered world. Knowledge has things pretty well under control, and the larger social order is stable and clearly valued. These assumptions no longer command ready assent — indeed, for some people, they are laughable. The outcome of this is that the prevailing mode for emotional satisfaction is moving away from dependence (since the reality will not support it) towards fight-flight (as evidenced in teacher militancy).

As professionals and politico-bureaucrats square off for a fight, we might wonder what will happen to everyone else. Parents and students must think that they are yo-yo's, with their emotions and motions up and down, with no control over events and the dawning realization that somebody has them on a string. The emotional turmoils of large human groups is awesome to behold, and we may well feel powerless to do anything but watch while our children become mere weapons in the struggle.

There is something to be done and Loren Lind outlines it very clearly. As human groups get larger they become more remote from reality, they even begin to suppose that they themselves are reality (which is why students tend to feed the system — the system *is* reality). To avoid wasting untold human energy, countless dollars, on fights that should never take place, we must recognize that professionals and politicians alike need to be closely in touch with the reality of parents and children. Educational politics are largely fantasy — which does not mean that they are not powerful and energy consuming — and they must be brought back into relationship with reality, the reality they are supposed to mediate, the reality of children and society, and this can be done if, as Loren Lind says, reform happens "in the inner world and outer world at the same time, and the best chance for it to happen is in the local neighborhood."

Politics, if it is the activity by which citizens take care of their social arrangements, can only be true to itself if it builds on a neighborhood base. What is true of Toronto is true of Canada — in spite of all its dangers and limitations, the only humane base is the neighborhood. Instead of strengthening the locality, the neighborhood, power has been accumulated in the centre, after the model of the giant industrial corporation. No wonder Loren Lind has to describe *The Learning Machine*.

John Bremer
14 August 1974
Victoria, B.C.

Chapter 1

TWO SCHOOLS

The classroom has seven kinds of dictionaries, it is that well stocked. It has a record player with five head-sets, a projector, film strips, three sets of basal readers, and a TV set down the hall. The teacher is one of the school system's best. "She'll have those gaffers reading in no time," the vice-principal tells me.

A reading lesson. The class is seated on the floor. She finishes a picture of an owl, asks them for the first letter.

"An owl begins with an A," a child pipes.

"Oh, please don't speak out, Richard," she replies.

It was fine that he got it wrong. It was wrong that he spoke out. Another child is allowed to answer who has his hand up.

This is Dundas Street Public School.

The building is situated just east of Cabbagetown, between the Don River and the east end, in an area sometimes called Riverdale. The streetcar noses along Dundas Street West through the slush, poking its way past a few pre-World War II tenements, past the brown brick Don Mount Housing Project, past the May Birchard Apartments and Jimmy's Snack Bar and Groceries, then screeches northward on Broadview Avenue.

The neighborhood seems thrown together, gutted and

strung out to dry. An older woman in snowsuit and gum boots, a bright orange stop sign in her hand, shepherds children across Dundas.

"Is this Riverdale?" I ask.

"I don't know, I guess it is. I've lived here all my life, and I don't even know . . . It's hard to tell because they're always changing the zone things, you know."

A place to live. Half the children at Dundas transfer during the school year, mainly to and from other parts of the inner city. They are squeezed in, 30,775 to a square mile amid shops and institutions, compared to 13,470 a square mile in tree-swept North Toronto.

You can't miss Dundas School. The street opens to a large asphalt slab, a series of chain-link fences, a teachers' parking lot, and finally, a rambling three-storey building. The entranceway is steel and glass trimmed in creamy pink. Inside, to the left, is a planter of plastic plants. Straight through you can see an enclosed courtyard of shrubs and trees. A giant blue poster hangs in the lobby. "At Dundas It's Happiness," it says.

School starts at 9. Children barely four trail their older brothers and sisters, feet squeaking in half-packed snow. One in six has no father living at home, and one in twelve has a father at home without work. Almost half of them are the sons and daughters of Toronto's working poor — labourers, truck drivers, waiters, porters, warehouse workers — people at the bottom end of Professor Bernard Blishen's socio-economic scale. They are not, for the most part, immigrant children, though among them they speak 24 languages besides English. Yet as Toronto schools go, their immigrant quotient is low. They are mostly of Anglo-Saxon stock, Canadians for many generations.

To begin a study of schooling in Toronto, I spent five

Two Schools

days at Dundas, and another five at John Ross Robertson. Neither school exists in a typically middle class neighborhood. Dundas reflects the disarray of the inner city, and John Ross Robertson the gentle splendor of affluent North Toronto. Two schools, tied to a central core of government, an institutional enclave of the mind, in which skills are taught and values are passed down. How are they different? How are they alike?

John Ross Robertson, a namesake to the founder of the now defunct *Toronto Telegram*, has the sunniness depicted so well in *Off to School*, one of the readers used at Dundas. John Ross Robertson is a colonial red brick building with white trim, a large front door that is painted white, and tall white spruces along the front walkway. Inside, the school looks just as schools should look, clean, cheery.

The two schools are only 4½ miles apart, but the social and economic distance is infinitely greater. You have to measure that distance with tangibles such as a $30,000-a-year difference in take-home pay. You have to see the contrasts in terms of two-car homes versus walk-up flats, vacations in Spain versus a *Star Fresh Air Fund* summer camp, skiing at Collingwood versus sledding down into the fence along the Don Valley Parkway.

The social landscape of schooling in Toronto varies from rugged to sublime. But the school system makes a studied effort to compensate for that. Both schools were well supplied with audiovisuals, books and teachers. The inner city funding program gave Dundas School a richer staff-pupil ratio and more money for supplies, counsellors and teachers' aides. But for all that, performance was sharply different, as judged by standardized exams, those monitors of public schooling.

Reading scores that both principals showed me had Dundas lagging far behind. More than one third of John Ross Robertson's top grade were comprehending above grade level; one ninth at Dundas' top grade were above grade level. In vocabulary, every other child at John Ross Robertson had command of words above their grade level; at Dundas, only one in 24 measured up that well. The Board of Education refused itself a full look at such schools, as we shall see in Chapter 5.

But a result was that children at Dundas and at six other inner city schools were twice as likely to be streamed into programs for slow learners than children in most other parts of town, a finding of the Every Student Survey of 1970. One further item of note is that seven at John Ross Robertson transferred out that year to private schools; none did at Dundas.

The inner city funding program barely compensates for all the handicaps of inner city schooling. One third of all the teaching staff at Dundas, for example, was new to the job that September. "With the exception of the year before last," the vice-principal, Dorothy Gossling, told me, "in the five years that I've been here, the smallest number of teachers to leave each year was 14." John Ross Robertson had only one new teacher.

Dundas coped with 42 non-English-speaking immigrant children; John Ross Robertson was to get its only three that next week, when a Danish professor's three children were expected to enroll.

Dundas had no organized community involvement at the school, except for several classroom volunteers, and four paid teachers' aides. John Ross Robertson has not one, but *two* parent organizations. Its principal, James Harvey, said with no great relish that JRR already was a "community school," he wouldn't think of instituting something new without consulting the parents. From all appearances, parents at Dundas simply let school keep, coming in only for open house, teacher interviews, or when there's trouble.

Principal George Baker held a public meeting in the fall of 1971 to hear parents' views about a new $30,000 adventure playground. Fewer than a dozen came. Earlier, without consulting the community, the Board had made way for this playground by buying and destroying 17 homes.

One final, distressing comparison. Dundas School stands in an area identified by Dr. Ursula Anderson of the Hospital for Sick Children as a high risk area, which means simply that babies born here stand a high chance of early death. The northern part of town is a low risk area, and the difference is 17 deaths for every 1,000 births. The possibility of survival at birth is 2$^1/_2$ times greater in North Toronto than it is along Dundas Street east of the Don.

I had selected Dundas and John Ross Robertson much at random. I knew nobody at either of them. I wanted inner city and North Toronto schools of similar size, but after visiting Dundas I couldn't find any that big in North Toronto. So I settled on one of the largest, JRR. Both schools were too large by either principal's estimate. Dundas had 841 pupils, John Ross Robertson 632.

Almost any comparison becomes a contrast in the environs and objective performance of these two schools.

Yet inside their doors the sharp differences melted into subtleties. At Dundas and at John Ross Robertson, education comes in what appears to be much the same package. I found both places wrapped snugly in the middle class etiquette of schooling. But at each school the wrapping had a different effect, depending on the interplay of school and community.

At upper middle class John Ross Robertson, the social and academic discipline seemed aimed at achievement. Some would fail, but their failure seemed small sacrifice to the enterprise that would allow so many to achieve what was called "excellence." "Whether it's democratic or not," one inner city vice-principal told me, "many of our leaders are coming from the north end schools." The disciplines made some kind of sense in that culture, with that prospect.

At lower working class Dundas Street, the discipline was clearly geared to social control. The task was to bring the unruly into line, the uncultured up to par, the slow learner up to average. "Maybe," one inner city principal confessed, "we get so overly concerned in dealing with those difficult kids who are disturbing the classes and making life difficult for the teacher and the other kids, that we are spending a disproportionate time on those kind." The feeling was that the poor had to be brought up to middle class standards before "excellence" was even in question. If some went so far as to succeed, that only showed they could do it if they really tried.

These forces coloured the atmosphere of schooling; you picked it up in the tiny nuances as well as the gross statistics. A facile conclusion would be that the system worked at John Ross Robertson, while at Dundas Street it failed. Quite otherwise: it worked at both schools.

A Grade 1 classroom at John Ross Robertson. It is a customary hodgepodge of colour. Cut-outs, paintings, writing displays, book-racks, chalkboard designs, listening terminal and earphones, autumn centres and seed centres, a whole range of alcoves and tiny nooks — these are the surroundings for a small fleet of tables and chairs. It varies little from the 240 other Grade 1 classrooms throughout the city.

A sign on the east wall:

>Hi! Welcome to Room 2
>   Our Class
>We have 27 children in our class,
>16 are boys and 11 are girls.
>Our teacher is Mrs MacIntyre.

> We like to play and work
> together. We are learning to read
> and print.

The children enter at 9, eager to continue their pumpkin-shaped books on their Thursday trip to the Horton Tree Farm. At the appropriate moment, the teacher begins singing and clapping, the children put their books on the rack and join her in a lively march around the room, hopping, going backwards, skipping or creeping as she directs. It ends in a huddle at Mrs MacIntyre's feet, the place for a 45-minute variety-packed exercise, that entails some talk, much listening, and much sitting cross-legged, with hands in lap.[1]

A boy named Peter tells how he sleeps in the attic with his brother, and they hear the squirrels scratching inside the ceiling. "Are you going to have some men come and take them out?" teacher asks.

Bewilderment breaks across Peter's face. He smiles, then frowns.

"They're looking for a warm place to spend the winter," she adds, "and if they make their nest there they might be a nuisance?"

He nods exuberantly. "Yeah," and takes his seat.

The children hear the proper way to take your bike through an intersection — always with the green light, always on foot. And how to brush your teeth, always downward for the top ones, upward for the lower jaw. The teacher says brightly: "You brush them the way they grow; if they grow up, you brush them up."

She breaks into a song. A boy points to a song written on a paper pumpkin. "One little, two little, three little witches . . ." they sing, racism having been edited out. "O Canada" follows, everyone standing, and then the Lord's Prayer, in deference to the *Schools Administration Act*.

[1] Names of teachers and pupils are changed.

It is show-and-tell time. A double line of children forms at the front, each child clutching something he brought from home. There's a miniature aqualung diver; a campaign pin, a soft drink truck with a Canada Dry decal on the back; a sack of marigold seeds; a toy bulldozer; a bright handbag from Peru; a paper snake made in China; an ear of corn.

The teacher goes into a lesson on the capital J. Her voice is richly sing-song. "Little j dooooooowwwwn in the basement, do you see?" The children have grown sullen. At 9:45 they go to their desks to print their J's over a full page of their copy tablet, including a row of *Jack* and *Jill*.

She then teaches them the sound of J. Taking two puppets in hand, one Jack, one Jill, she makes them jump. Surprise! Jump sounds just like Jack and Jill at the beginning. She asks those with names starting the same way to come to the front, as do two John's, a Jamie, a Jennifer, and alas, a Geoffrey. She explains the difference. Two of them are allowed to be Jack and Jill. Cards are distributed to all, some with pictures of things starting with J, others with other pictures. Jack and Jill are to pick out persons who are to say whether or not their picture starts with J, and if so to put it on the blackboard, and if not, to stand it on the chalk rail.

The children begin to fidget. Teacher: "If you can't keep your card quiet, we'll give it to someone else." She urges Jack and Jill to choose someone who's been sitting up nicely. Now she wavers between sing-song and whispering, playing her voice to keep the class at a tolerable level of attention. An underlying gutsiness outlasts her fatigue and sustains the wordplay. She praises those who sit straight, promises them rewards, corrects those who forget. "Straight back, a quiet hand, and legs crossed in front." The perfect Grade 1 child.

The classroom, then, isn't free and open, as the official rhetoric goes. It's tightly orchestrated. The Dick-and-Jane world handed down to their parents has become a Jack-and-

Two Schools

Jill world of their own. There is a lot of movement, most of it purposeful.

The more I visited the schools, the more I became aware that the new order of schooling relies on a sophistication — and sometimes an inversion — of the former methods of control. Strapping children is no longer in vogue, even though surveys have shown that most Ontario teachers believe it ought to be permitted. Progressive teachers no longer force young children to sit still all the time, only part of the time. Lavish chaos, or at least a lively disorder has come to replace the classroom decor based on five straight rows. The new regime rests on less obvious techniques.

Part of the new control tactics lies hidden in the very process of making choices. As Eleanor Smollett pointed out in the January 1974 issue of *This Magazine*, school exerts a control in the modern setting by forcing multiple choice answers. By learning to make choices involving no real human content, as you might choose between *Tide* and *Fab*, the child gets caught up in a circular activity that leads away from self-realization. It leads toward a mechanical choice-making model, required for the stability of the established social and economic system outside the school. The child, to use Ms Smollett's words, is "kept in control with subtle precision."

There is also a heavy emotional barrage laid down to insure that a very limited range of human experience emerges in the classroom. Schooling takes place in the happy-go-lucky land of Jack-and-Jill. What's often strived for is a hyped euphoria, an artificial ecstasy, that offers learning at the expense of nine-tenths of what the children know.

In a Grade 4 classroom at Dundas School the teacher keeps the pupils in tidy rows. A portly, proper woman, she has written the rules on the blackboard in her own neat longhand: "1. We must be quiet in class . . . " Math assignments are spelled out on another blackboard, and all 27 pupils seem studiously at work. Nobody talks above muted tones, including the teacher.

Then at 11 o'clock sharp, in bursts the Poet. Long hair, wide eyes, a slapdash manner, he lays it to them in an upbeat preacher's chant. Today's topic is concrete poetry, just as last week's lesson was sound poetry. He shakes off the pedestrian mood of the class with one big shrug, and the children look scared. But they obligingly bend crayons to paper, copying from the blackboard the designs he tells them not to copy.

"All I'm trying to do is break down their idea of poetry," he told me later, adding more thoughtfully, "The only way it can really happen, though, is through individual attention." That is one thing, of course, they cannot expect.

The Poet is sent here by the Inner City Angels, a volunteer organization dedicated to bringing culture to those without it, and Principal Baker thinks it a good thing. He also supported a bid by the National Survey Bureau to test toothpaste flavors on his five-year-olds for 75 cents a head (the money would go to them), and a request by Professor Harvey Narrol, a behavioral psychologist, to let his students try out their tests on 80 of his pupils. The school, having no parent organization, is a good place to experiment. Principal Baker speaks well of the Poet coming in, because his children need all the enrichment they can get.

The Poet makes his way around the class as the children try their hand at concrete poetry. He has a habit of clacking his heels on the floor and swinging around fast. He did this to Robert Katsouloulos.

"What are you making?" the Poet asked.

"I forgot," Robert replied, very honest.

"You forgot? Why don't you write 'forgot' and then start words with those letters of all the things you forgot?" and he clacks his heels and is off.

Robert then writes his name in shaky letters with blue crayon. He draws a line around it, and a wavy line at the top. "It's a shark."

Many children are doing underwater things. The teacher, too, seems at sea. She walks up behind Teddy, stoops to view his brilliant letter collage, and moves on wordlessly.

At 11:30 time's up. The Poet shouts goodbye to a quiet room, and he is gone. The teacher has two children mop up the blackboard and sets them all doing maths. Robert Katsouloulos is happy. He copies $32 \times 2 = 64$ in his notebook. I ask how he does it.

"You put them in boxes," he explains.

"What do you mean?"

"Well, you have two boxes with two in, and three boxes with two in. That's 64."

The noon buzzer rings, and he slaps shut his workbook.

But Robert doesn't run to the door. The teacher holds on to her class. "I need a volunteer from each row when you're sitting up straight." She appoints one from each row to pick up the math books. "Oh, I like the way Row 3 is getting ready to go neat," she comments, inspiring straight backs along Row 3. She allows the girls to line up first: "I let the boys line up first at recess."

She chats pleasantly with two rows of sex-segregated children until intuition tells her it's time to open the door. They merge with similarly sex-segregated rows in the hallway.

The vice-principal at Dundas, who has since become a principal at another school, told me that girls file past the girls' washroom, the boys past the boys', so that any child may slip out of line on the way to the playground. The school discourages using the washroom during the lunch hour play period.

Discipline at Dundas School had a harder edge than at John Ross Robertson. It wasn't that the inner city school laid more formal emphasis on obedience, only that the emphasis seemed loaded. School was seen as these children's one big chance of making it out of poverty to lives of middle class plenty. Uptown, by contrast, the heaviness of the rules was lightened by a general feeling that the kids had good chances of making it. The atmosphere was less charged with raw need. School regulations could be taken as a game to be played rather than a gauntlet to be run.

But at both schools, although with differing effects, the pupils learned predictable responses.

Handraising, for example.

One kind of handraising occurs in response to the sound of a certain chime or chord. Tacked onto the piano in a Dundas School junior kindergarten were the words: "C chord is signal for attention — children place hands on shoulders and listen." This teacher had the good grace to make it a mere breather, like a referee calling time. But in another classroom a bright-eyed young teacher wielded the routine as if her life depended on it, as perhaps it did.

She used a toy xylophone, carrying it around the room, banging it at brief intervals, having less and less effect. "Hands on heads, not one muscle moving," she finally shouted. "All right, I'm going to let someone that's sitting up straight with their bottom on the rug come up and choose a picture that starts like Mother, Pat or Cat."

Later, when I asked the teacher where she learned to use the xylophone, she told me it was in Teachers' College. "They taught us a lot of music to use with kindergarten classes, but I wasn't very good at it."

The vice-principal explained, "They learn at Teachers' College to avoid talking, to not be talking to the children all the time, and so they do these things with the xylophone. Some of them take it too far."

Once at another school I joined a five-year-old with head-sets to hear a story on the record player. Suddenly his hands flew up. I looked around. Hands were going up all over the room. Then I saw the teacher at the piano; the chord had been struck. Nothing this mere five-year-old might have been doing could match the compelling sound of the C chord. When I queried the principal, she was surprised at my naivete. It was something kindergarten teachers just did as a way of getting attention.

A child trained to respond instantly to a chime has been conditioned to the fundamentals of schooling. It is within this framework that a public education can begin. The raised hands of later lessons are a ritualized tribute to the supremacy of the system that makes education possible.

Competition is still a dominant tool for motivation, despite the precepts of Ontario's bible of progressive education, the Hall-Dennis Report. But the differing functions of competition at these two schools seemed to reflect the prospective role of the children in society.

At John Ross Robertson, competition seemed aimed at the task at hand. At least it worked to keep many of them straining for excellence. After an initial training in handraising and sitting still, pupils in the upper grades fought for high marks. Some got hurt, but at least it produced the achievement acceptable to both teacher and parent. And to children versed in middle class values, explicit social rewards seemed worth it.

A high school principal once explained to me why the system ought to award diplomas every two years: "It seems to me a kid is playing a ballgame here and getting no rewards for it until the end," he told me. Wasn't learning its own reward? I asked. "Well, yes," he quickly agreed, "the reward of playing hockey is playing hockey, but it's a heck of a lot better reward if you get a trophy for it." And one of his Grade 13 students, a former student council president, told me: "Every student's after that little piece of paper. . . . The majority of us, I'd say about 75 percent, don't want to go to class, but we do it because we have to, and because of that little piece of paper. . . . Actually, most of us see it as a jailhouse."

At Dundas School, the competition I observed rarely rose above the level of behavioral control. Whatever the reason, the primary tool of schooling was seldom used for anything beyond getting children to keep their places. Asking them to compete for achievement seemed somehow mean; these were, after all, "inner city kids." But if they behaved themselves they might make it.

To get some idea of the similarities and differences, let's look again at some classrooms.

Out behind the main building at John Ross Robertson in a portable classroom, a teacher was giving a spelling test to 27 pupils. The teacher called out words like "Coronado" and "evaporation," his students wrote them down. Then he tested them by calling on students to spell them aloud. Loud whispers, sighs and gasps. Great groans from the losers. At the very end, he had his pupils stand and call out their scores, starting at the lowest. Five remained standing with perfect scores.

I asked why they tried so hard. He laid it to their wanting to excel among peers, and to strong home pressures. He told me that 15 of his 27 were superior students. Four lagged behind, and I soon saw it happen.

One girl tries to do fractional equivalents, page 65 of *Mathematics 6*, the textbook co-authored by one of the teacher's superiors in the system, math director W. Winston Bates. She is baffled by the problem: $1/5 + 2/3 = $. This, the book says, is an uncompleted mathematical sentence. Complete it. She can't get it, so he sends her to the side board. She is too rattled to think straight, a tall, round-tummied girl in jeans, tittering and scared. He brings her over to his front blackboard, and lays out very clearly how one can find the proper equivalent of $1/5$. It equals $2/10$ and $3/15$. That settled, she goes back to her side board and tries to raise $2/3$ to a denominator of 15 herself, but fails. She writes down a number, stands back, starts to go to her seat, comes back, erases it, tries again until teacher tells her to stand back. She has it wrong. Again he helps her raise $2/3$ to a denominator of 15. She finally gets it and sits down giggling.

The teacher said he's lucky to have only 27 students, but even that is too many for the currently fashionable goals of open education. So he offers a highly structured program; his pupils learn what he says they will. "I don't argue for this system, really," he said. "But it's so difficult, even with 27 students, to give individual attention. I've tried to work in groups, and let them organize their own learning. It's great for some kids, but as an end product, at the end of the year, I sit back and I ask myself, what have I done for these kids? Have they gained a body of knowledge? I'm more satisfied that they have when I direct their learning myself."

There is the question of competition. He explained to me that the children are far more critical of each other than he is of them. "For a child that is not particularly good," he told me, "they'll tear him apart." It was enough to make me remember Piggy in William Golding's novel *Lord of the Flies*, crushed under a boulder by his peers.

I asked him whether this general animosity isn't fanned by the competitiveness of the school scene. "Yes, but even when there isn't any competition, kids can be brutal."

Kids can be brutal. I visited a Grade 4 class at the same school, in which the children learned to compete. The teacher put her class through its paces in tensely ordered fashion. Pupils rarely got out of line and never out of hand. I soon discovered children going to the front of the room to push cardboard turtles along tracks made of strings. There were four turtles, yellow, orange, red and gray. Each turtle, I soon learned, was sponsored by a "turtle house." She selected children for these houses earlier in the year, and the problem of discipline was then well in hand.

"It works wonderfully well," she explained. "They get points for work well done, for good behavior, and exceptionally creative activities. Only very rarely do I move a turtle back for poor performance. They get to move it forward about this far (she measures three inches with her fingers) and I keep watch to see that nobody cheats, but they're pretty good at watching each other that way.

"I keep a record on this chart each week to see which turtle house is ahead, and at the end of the year we will see who wins, and I will give each of them a little prize."

One of the turtles was already hopelessly behind. That house, I was told, included a "deviant" child. The orange turtle house seemed to be doing best, and so the teacher allowed it to leave first for recess. The teacher assured me her method was not unique; another teacher next door used rockets, she said, "but I prefer turtles because they're slow."

Slow or fast, the fact that it worked so smoothly shows how implicit the competitive factor was in the upper middle class school by Grade 4. But the same kind of technique also worked at Dundas, though at a deeper level of brutality, with orderliness as its key objective.

At Dundas School a starchily dressed young man just out of Toronto Teachers' College took a small group of Grade 2 children behind a partition to drill their reading. "Nice and straight," his voice boomed from behind a bookcase. "I don't call on anyone that's not sitting up nice and straight." Later, as his class emerged for Crayon work, he told them, "The person that lines up best will get the piece of paper I've folded." They line up straight, making little flourishes for that piece of paper he folds slowly, deliciously. They stand at attention, all eyes to the fore. Finally he gives the word: "I think I'm going to give it to Morgan this morning. He looks very nice."

Still earlier, in a Grade 1 room at Dundas, the class of 26 sat on a blue rug, legs crossed in regulation style, bodies writhing, hands waving, elbows poking, minds deviously at work. It was reading time. The teacher, also fresh out of Teachers' College with a primary certificate, explained she would show them a picture, and they were to choose words printed on the blackboard to describe them. At the first flash, a chorus of voices: "Pumpkin."

"Let me see some hands please," she replied, not delighted. "Now I will only hear from people who have their hands up," she repeated a moment later. And again: "I'm not asking Alice because she called out. I'm asking Frank."

The children get the message. Several boys who couldn't care less sat at the edge of the unhappy circle, gladly letting it go on without them. Sally fidgeted until she touched off another response: "Sally, would you please go back to your desk and put your head down." And a plump girl in black braids crawled defiantly along the edge of the rug until the teacher handed her over to the vice-principal. The others fought it out, doing their feverish best to get attention in the prescribed fashion, with varying degrees of success. The game shifted to word flashcards. The first card reads "Comes."

"Colour," shouted one girl.

"I'm not going to answer you if you don't have your hands up," the teacher replied.

Hands flew wildly until she chose a likelier prospect.

"Come," said the girl.

"Comessss," replied the teacher.

At Dundas School one morning, tiny Rachel of Macedonia, scarcely in kindergarten, hears a big woman boom at her in the hallway, "What's your room number?" and doesn't know and can't understand. Her older sister tugs her through the hallway chaos into Julia Hung's junior kindergarten classroom. That morning Rachel gets to paint, and she fills her whole paper with great gobs of black. The aide asks what color it is, hoping to teach her something.

"Can you say black?"

"Black," says Rachel.

Raymond, an Anglo, struts around the room knocking over blocks, not liking it when Jimmy comes in the door late and a girl sighs, "Big Jim."

"I'm Big Ray," says Raymond, thumping his chest.

And a small Greek boy with a left eyelid that droops sits forlorn beside a pile of blocks, unable to move until Mrs Hung kneels beside him and asks him to find a truck. He does. She praises him. "Now say 'truck'," she says, getting very close. He looks away in pain. "Look at me," she calls, grasping him gently and holding her head straight in front of his. His head droops, he mutters the word, feels a shower of praise on the back of his neck. Later she comes by again and hands him a block. He puts it gingerly atop another. "Very good," she exclaims. He puts another block beside it. More praise. Then he snatches a toy car, puts it in a corner of blocks. "Now you have a garage," she says, triumphant. "Good for you (she says his name), you make me so happy today." It is praise freely given, and he later gets to ride the big tricycle around the playlot, a brave smile on his face. But at the end of the week he's to be transferred out; his parents are moving several blocks north, which puts him in another school, and Spiro's life again depends on his getting another exceptional teacher.

At Dundas Street, John Ross Robertson, and the other

143 schools in the system, the children are learning.

The small Greek boy stood a chance with Mrs Hung because of her warmth, despite the little note about the C chord tacked to the piano. And the round-tummied girl in the maths class probably would learn to do fractions some day.

But the framework for learning at either school set the limits and established the priorities. In one community, school may turn out successes, in another, failures. But whether they succeed or fail at their official lessons, the children certainly will learn schooling.

It is 9:30 a.m., classtime for 60 certified elementary teachers who are taking a five-week summer course offered by the Ministry of Education at Toronto's west end Humberside Collegiate Institute. They file quietly into an auditorium, facing a small podium and a large black blackboard. This course and four others will raise them on the salary scale by $400 next year, which is mainly why they are taking it. It is a class in measurement and evaluation. This is where they will learn to categorize children, put their classes onto frequency polygons and histograms, measure their teaching by the off-whack leanings of the bell shape curve. It is good stuff to know among the pedagogically alert in the Toronto system. A Toronto elementary school principal is the lecturer. Having heard about the median the day before, they will learn about mode today. He writes a line of numbers on the board: 0,1,1,2,3, 3,3,4,4,5,6,6. "Mode is simply the score that appears most frequently," he says. Then: 0,1,1,2,3,3,3,4,4,5,5,5,6,6. "This has two numbers appearing most frequently, therefore it is said to have two modes, or it's bimodal."

He does another, which has three equally frequent numbers.

"Trimodal," the teachers shout.

"No," he replies. "It's multimodal. If we have more

than two, we just lump them all together and call it multimodal. . . . When the modes of the bimodal are numerically adjacent, we just give the one mode by averaging them out. You can draw a picture of it so you can tell what it looks like." He draws this:

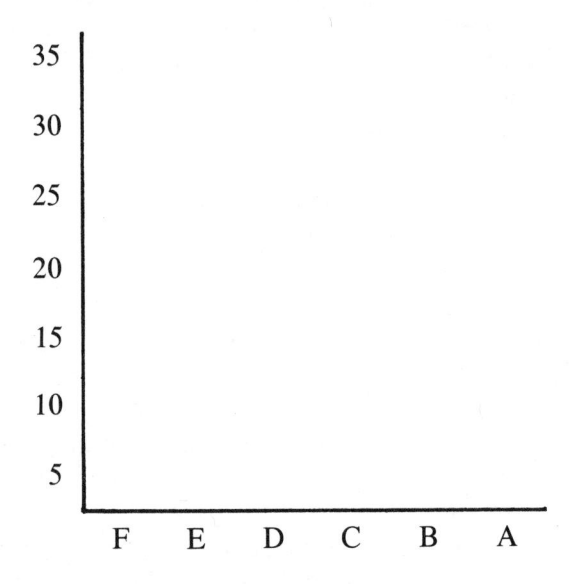

```
35 |
30 |
25 |
20 |
15 |
10 |
 5 |
   |_____
     F   E   D   C   B   A
```

"That affords us a picture of what our scores look like." Then he writes the word "histogram" on the blackboard. It is made the same way but with bars. He does it. A woman teacher wants to know why there are more below C than above. "This distribution tells you you're working with a group slanting to the lower end. That's why we're doing this kind of thing, to tell you what kind of group you're working with." He draws a multimodal frequency polygon on the blackboard:

A rich baritone voice from a row of laughing teachers at the very back: "Might not that multimodal result just mean you have a rotten test?"

"I don't like that personal inference," says the lecturer, completely serious. "You could have a split group, too." This question breaks his flow. He recovers with an explanation that a representative group should not be bimodal. He then shifts to the uses of mean, median and mode.

"Will you repeat that?" a woman calls. He repeats, slowly recitative: "The mode is useful when a quick, approximate measure of concentration is needed."

Sixty pens tilt dutifully to paper, there is a quiet, studied feeling, a sense of relief at lecture sustained, as these incontrovertibly true and sensible sentences sink onto paper. They are learning to become better teachers.

Chapter 2

THE RISE OF NEW CANADIANISM

Joyce Chu sat in her living room near Ogden Public School telling me how it was with Chinese children growing up in Canada. "This little one there," she said, glancing at Ian, her six-year-old, "he knows only a little Chinese. As soon as he goes to school he gets only English, he plays with English friends, and the first thing you know he forgets Chinese."

The words came plain and blunt through an interpreter. Joyce Chu spoke Cantonese. The setting as much as the words got through to me, along with the glowing family portraits they handed around, the big Chinese posters on the wall. It wasn't just sentiment; the culture was something deeper than that. She offered me Burton's Merry English Assorted Biscuits and a cup of coffee on a small stool.

"Most of the children say they hate Chinese . . . they don't respect the parents when they learn English . . . they lose what we give."

A calm, motherly lady, an immigrant from Hong Kong, Joyce Chu turns out Mister Leonard pants and jackets at $1.10 apiece on an industrial sewing machine the company has let her keep in the living room. Yuehong, her husband, is a cook at Old Ed's Restaurant. He leans against a big hi-fi amplifier, reads the *Shing Wah Daily News*, says little. "When the children talk among themselves, they use English," Joyce Chu was saying. "They only use Chinese when they want something from us. Most parents don't speak English. We talk to them in Chinese and they don't understand."

Joyce Chu, mother of five, is vice-chairman of the Chinese Parents' Association, a little group rallied by Trustee Dan Leckie to press for multicultural rights in Toronto's central core. (After all, 75 per cent of the children at Ogden, and 95 per cent of the children at Orde Street Public School, are from Chinese homes.) She is one of a swiftly awakening lot of non-Anglo-Saxons who want their native languages taught at the public schools. It is a wildly excessive demand, by Ontario standards, and as I write this their success or failure is still in doubt.

Toronto's programs for immigrant children have the basic aim of adapting these new arrivals to the language and culture of Anglo-Saxon Toronto. It has taken a variety of forms, from neo-progressive to straight-out traditional, but never has it gone beyond a rather crude version of cultural assimilation. This chapter will show how it happened in Toronto.

When Edgar Wright, director of research, did his Every Student Survey in 1970, he found that fully 40 per cent of Toronto's students spoke something other than English as their mother tongue. One fourth had been born outside Canada, and their birth places rivaled in diversity the United Nations itself. Some children even said they came from countries nobody could locate, such as Popimento, Sango, Funigulo and Ngumbi. Give or take a nationality, the Toronto school system contains enough diversity to offer a world of cultural enrichment to all its students.

It has scrupulously ignored this diversity. Even though two in five speak languages other than English as their mother tongue, only English and (in rare cases) French have been the languages of instruction. Over 10,000 speak Italian, but none can learn to read it at an elementary school despite the fact that over 4,000 parents have requested it.[1] Another 4,000 speak Portuguese, 3,000 Greek, 2,700 Chinese, 1,200 Polish. Except for the 14 per cent who get private instruction in their native tongues, their heritage is swiftly fading.

The policy has been called a New Canadian Program. It is in fact cultural assimilation. Toronto has British traditions to which its school system clings with undying faith. The French fact lies somewhere deep in its origins, too, and it recognizes this as the price of being Canadian. But the full variety and cultural diversity have burst upon it late in history, and Toronto somehow hasn't got used to it.

Toronto was a Seneca Indian village at first, located at the sound end of a trail leading southward from Lake Huron to Lake Ontario. Its name was Teiaiagon. The French made it a trading post in the early 1700's but lost it to the English in 1759. Thirty years later John Graves Simcoe made it the capital of Upper Canada, but by the time the Americans sacked it in 1813, only 800 souls lived here. Its first mayor was a rebel, William Lyon Mackenzie. He led the 1837 uprising against the Family Compact and had to flee to New York State after a battle at Montgomery's Tavern on Yonge Street. At Confederation in 1867, Toronto regained the capital status it lost briefly to Kingston, and steadily grew into a major city. The British, the United

[1] The Every Student Survey of 1970 by Edgar Wright, entitled *Student's Background and its Relationship to Class and Programme in School*, lists 44 mother-tongue languages spoken by Toronto students; 35 per cent spoke Italian. The requests for foreign language instruction were enumerated in a city-wide questionnaire sent to elementary school parents in 1973. Two thirds of the pupils' parents replied, and of those, 4,060 wanted Italian taught, 3,049 wanted German, 2,549 wanted Spanish, 1,536 wanted Greek, 1,139 wanted Chinese and 952 wanted Portuguese.

Empire Loyalist, and then the Irish potato famine refugee filled out Toronto as a late-blooming industrial centre.

Until World War II, despite its varied history, Toronto the Good was still officially white Anglo-Saxon, if not wholly Protestant. Major immigrant waves had already arrived. The Irish had long since settled Cabbagetown, a strong Jewish migration from eastern Europe moved into Kensington, and Italians from Rome and northern Italy got a foothold in the great flat belt around Christie Pits.

The British who tried to defend it in 1813 were trying to defend it still. But the past 30 years have tipped the balance. And although the city was rapidly filling with non-Anglo-Saxon, mainly Catholic and southern European immigrants, for the first 20 of those 30 years, the Toronto Board of Education seemed hardly to notice. The attitude back then was strict paternalism, the secret wish that immigrants, if they must come, would silently grow up and be like us. Cecil Charles Goldring, director of education, studied the "immigrant problem" in 1951, only to find that his school principals found these strangers were timid, they clung tenaciously to native customs, they had trouble forming friendships, they were distressed. "Unusual names, as 'Wolfgang,' make the pupils self-conscious," one principal said. "With parental consent we changed his name to Wilfred." It was a common solution.

Goldring, who once wrote a Grade 8 text called *We Are Canadian Citizens*, seemed determined not to overreact. He ended his report by quoting the principal who said, "I think the less fuss about the matter the better. They should merge with the general population as soon as possible." The trustees' only response was to thank the Home and School Association of Greater Toronto for its work in making immigrants feel at home. That was 1951.

The turning point came in 1965. An immigrant study by

the Toronto Board's Research Department, *Immigrants and Their Education*, piqued the liberal conscience with the first sustained look at Toronto's newly arrived children. Those "limited" in their ability to use English numbered 4,843, twice the number that had arrived in the previous 10½ months. "It has reached a point where there are Greeks learning Italian so that they can get along in Toronto," the report chided. "Our school system and most of the schools have tended to maintain themselves in a 'splendid isolation' waiting for the children from other lands to adjust to our city, our ways and our classrooms. . . . Only the tremendous variety of immigrants, their mobility, and the continuing influx have prevented sharply defined ghettos from developing."

Much of Metro Toronto's post-war expansion came from southern Europe, Hong Kong, Great Britain and the West Indies. The new arrivals grouped themselves loosely in mixed neighborhoods, unlike the tightly packed ghettos of many American cities.[2] Italians took to the southwestern quartile of the inner city, at first containing themselves south of College Street but rapidly pressing northward across St. Clair and Eglinton, finally spilling into suburban North York. They make up well over one fourth the foreign-born population of the public school system, giving the schools a major Catholic ingredient. The Italians came mainly from Calabria and Sicily; they were rural people, farmers and manual laborers, craftsmen and tradesmen. In Toronto they swelled the construction trades. The Greeks at first took to the restaurant business. They settled mainly along Danforth Avenue, venturing into Toronto's eastern half, an area that was strongly white Anglo-Saxon Protestant — and still is. The Chinese created Chinatown just

---

[2] When Anthony Richmond surveyed the householders of Metro Toronto in 1971 he found that while half had been born outside Canada, their settlements here were loose and fluid. Their mobility appeared to be a tribute both to their own initiative and to the rapid growth of the city.

north-east of city hall, then pushed westward toward Spadina Avenue, hard pressed by court and municipal office buildings and commercial developments. Today they stand to be the next proprietors of that old market area of Kensington. Here the Portuguese still hold sway, but they too are pressing westward toward High Park, where Polish, Ukrainian and German nationalities predominate. Shops along Roncesvalles Avenue have clerks who speak German but no English, and West Park Secondary School in that area has no smoking signs in five languages. The West Indians set up their food shops and travel bureaus in along Bathurst Street north of Bloor; for them begins the long, slow migration northward, while more recent newcomers fill in vacancies downtown.

The Board of Education could hardly ignore them; it acted conspicuously, and with a fine sense of political timing.

In 1966, when criticism began to mount, the Board of Education could point to what it had begun to do. It had started one completely new New Canadian school, it had sent teachers into 20 schools to work full-time exclusively with immigrant children, it had requested the largest study to date from its Research Department. The remnant of New Canadian classes that kicked along sporadically before 1965 was sharply re-valued. A bold new approach to immigrant education was begun. It was impressive enough to turn a liability into a blessing. By 1967, the *Globe and Mail* was saying of the new school for immigrants, "The Toronto Board of Education spends no other part of its budget so wisely."

Behind all this was a build-up of theory and research unequalled in other programs that the Board has adopted, and some of it might have been useful as a base to provide a much richer program for immigrant children. The Board, however, made sure it wouldn't be. It stripped the research of its subtleties, its hesitations, its suggestions for other approaches to immigrant education, and focussed on the one major approach the research suggested. This one approach, well suited to the political organization of the system, blanked out other prospects. It became the doctrine of New Canadianism.

Joseph Sterioff, a vibrant Macedonian, born and schooled in Cabbagetown, was the choice of Superintendent Norman Sweetman for principal of Main Street School, an experimental program for immigrant children that began in 1965. Sterioff still talks with feverish enthusiasm about what happened at Main Street. For him, he says, it started with a simple truth. This was the seemingly prosaic fact that language is just one facet of culture. He summed it up in the Kennedyesque rhetoric of the day: "A Greek is not a Greek because he has learned to speak the language of Greece; rather, he speaks the language of Greece because he is a Greek . . ."

It was so self-evident, when you thought about it. Joe Sterioff seemed embarrassed that it was so simple. But it made the world light up. On this insight he built the notion that the way to learn a language is to be submerged in its culture. "In short, the simple expedient of somehow getting the new immigrant school boy to sound, write or recognize the signals we use to represent our language is not going to do anything at all about his mastering the language, let alone his integrating the culture which developed it, into his own nervous system," he wrote at the time. "Invite him to the culture and he will acquire the language for himself, as well as the trappings that make it sensible."

So the problem of learning a language is not just a language problem; it is a cultural problem. The solution, said Sterioff, is to immerse the child in his new culture and offer him the language as a way of making sense of it. This was put more starkly by Joseph Gladstone, then a consultant at the school, who saw the inculcation of values as a key to language: "Provide the child with the need and the opportunity to internalize the value system of the culture and he will learn the language quickly and with understanding."[3]

This approach placed great emphasis on the chasm that separates one language from another. "Language is a manifestation of culture," the Research Department stated in *Immigrants and their Education*, "and exact translations from language to language are not possible." This gave administrators a way of coping that was at once sophisticated and reassuring. Obviously, the only way to bridge the gap was to immerse the newcomers totally in English; they were to start from ground zero.

Without ill will, almost coincidentally, immigrants became defined as problems. "A New Canadian child," said one official report in 1970, "is any child who is unable to function successfully in a regular school programme because his ethnic background reflects a culture other than our own." Instead of viewing these children as specially advantaged, it declared them handicapped. Their potential bilingualism became a stigma.

Senstitive to this, the New Canadian theorists paid backhanded tribute to immigrant cultures. Whenever Sterioff declared his approach would help the student "commit himself to our Canadian culture", he invariably added the phrase "without completely rejecting the culture he was born into"; but the program easily discarded the prepositional clause.

Sterioff, himself an immigrant's child, always seemed edgy about this. That New Canadianism became the theoretical base for immigrant education during this critical

[3] "An Experiential Approach to the Teaching of English as a Second Language," *English Language Teaching,* May, 1967.

decade was probably due more to the forces around him than to his own salesmanship. While Sterioff anticipated "the long process of distilling a common cultural pattern in which we can all take pride", he also saw virtue in "our legitimate cultural diversity" that could serve to "strengthen us against shocks." He added hopefully that "the creation of one pattern need not destroy internal individual differences."[4]

Such second thoughts were straws in the wind as the educational reformers of the 1960's swept into immigrant education.

The doctrine of New Canadianism emerged out of the loosely linked, liberal-progressive thinktank at the Educational Centre, whose resident philosopher was Mel Lafountaine. He impressed on Edgar Wright, Joe Sterioff and Joe Gladstone the interconnections of language and culture based on the literature of E.T. Hall and Edward Sapir, and going right back to Ludwig Wittgenstein's postulate: "Language is culture." Or rather, as Joe Sterioff put it in a booklet he authored on *English as a Second Language:* "Language is the noise of culture talking to itself."

This philosophy was admirably suited to several obvious priorities. For one thing, it complemented the Hall-Dennis neo-progressivism that was to supersede the dark ages of mechanical drills and curriculum-centred routines. It allowed — indeed, encouraged — teachers to put aside the mechanics of language on the presumption of going deep into the heart of things — into the culture itself. This

---

[4] A sentence by Sterioff that ought to be framed on the wall of every New Canadian classroom in seven languages: "If we foster this diversity, if we encourage free pluralistic development of languages and cultures, far from destroying our unity, they can be its principal ornament and strength. Any other course could be our undoing, for the elimination of differences pursued to the end can lead to the most fearful impoverishment of all — the sameness which is poverty of spirit."

was outlined in Sterioff's pamphlet. Far from being a mere system of tonal noises and grammatical structure, it says, language is the transfer of experience itself. "It is not a subject; but rather an interactive process which internalizes itself as part of the human organism's nervous system." And the best way into a new language is to explore the new culture it represents. "To achieve these ends, teachers must abandon the strictures of a binding curriculum, the sterility of a one-way information flow, and the stagnation of a stereotyped classroom environment."

In a time when the New Math was starting to bloom, New Canadianism partook of the same heady conceptualizations. The dull drills and the hated grammar would fall into place once a basic feel for the Canadian way of life had dawned.

This approach had practical attractions, too. The hiring of bilingual teachers and the grouping of pupils by nationality became unnecessary. The staff could be trained on a uniform basis; their instructions could be printed in a single teachers' guide.

And finally, the New Canadian program seemed to suit Toronto's multi-cultural pattern, especially in the east end. Toronto — at least to the Anglo-Saxon perception — had no hard-core ethnic ghettos. This meant no school was likely to get New Canadians of only one variety. A school might have clusters of Greeks, Portuguese, Italians and Chinese, making it difficult to give each nationality an appropriately bilingual teacher.

The solution was not to try. Administrators went queasy at the thought of untrammeled diversity.

The system, at any rate, chose to play it singlemindedly. If the new Canadian approach bulldozed all the alien languages under the fine top soil of schoolbook English, at least it did so with philosophical elegance and some convincing practical arguments.

In 1965, Joe Sterioff moved into Main Street with his team of eight teachers, and 72 non-English-speaking pupils. An inverted Tower of Babel, the entire school could be designed to his own specifications. He ordered 80 trapezoid tables instead of desks. His book supplies that first year cost $4,740; his audio-visual supplies $15,625. He also got 15 round tables for the teacher-pupil discussions over lunch, and six projection screens, one for each "communication area" (read classroom). There was also a language console with taped lessons to be heard in tandem with slide pictures flashed on a screen — Toronto's first. Main Street, Sterioff declared, was "a kind of laboratory for the child — he had experiences out there in the world, and he came to school to make sense of them."

Under Sterioff's two-year tenure, the school did not totally neglect native cultures. An open house featured lavish ethnic displays, described by Barrie Zwicker in *The Globe and Mail*: "An example of the imagination used by students and teachers is the Greek marketplace awnings, achieved by placing colored striping on long window blinds and raising the ends on poles. Colorful gourds are burned-out lightbulbs covered with papier mache. Turkish coffee will be brewed and served." Joe Sterioff ambled through the displays explaining to Zwicker his space-age dreams. "One hundred years from now we won't learn about a country from text books or even movies. Transportation will be so cheap that we'll simply travel there."

And so, in the winter of 1973, I visited Main Street School with Sterioff's visions ("Language is the fallout of one's culture"; "Motivation begins with the child, his interests, his play, his imagination") clanging in the back of my head. What I found was a sleepy little school full of folksiness and apologies. The glory — was it once there? — had gone sallow by five years of inattention and the thousand little repercussions that wear away at any experiment in the system.

Joseph Weare, a short, bespectacled man, fidgety and self-effacing, brought me into an office dominated by a huge glass-topped desk. It was the principal's office, and he was the principal. Weare answered a few of my questions; he was anxious to get on with a slide lecture about the school I was in, giving me Kodachrome examples of the flesh and blood specimens outside his door. Then he gave me a purple ditto sheet that introduced me to his staff and timetabled my day, including a chaperoned interview with six handpicked students. At noon he took me and Andy Pandoff, the guidance man, to a Chinese restaurant for lunch. Ordinarily, he said, the staff eats with the pupils.

It turned out that Main Street was quite an ordinary school, small, sheltered and pleasant. There were now 187 pupils. The ratio of pupils to teachers was only 15 to 1. It still was exceptionally well outfitted in audiovisuals. It was still a happy school. Angela Boltsis, 15, born in Russia to Greek parents, came back to visit a year after she left in February 1972. In Grade 9 then at Oak Park Junior High School, she liked Main Street better. She liked the dances, the trips, the essays, the art. Main Street still was, by Toronto standards, a very small school. Weare and his teachers did their best to accommodate children, make strangers feel at home, blunt the edges of competitive schooling. There was dancing twice a week. A buddy system gave students of the same nationality a sense of security. But despite the obvious goodwill, the program itself was nothing like the pedagogical idealism propounded by Sterioff and Gladstone. The school now used testing; it stressed reading and writing rather than just oral English in vocabulary; it proliferated drills and paper work; and it taught all rudiments as subjects rather than gleaning them, as the literature says, from culture. The outings took place, but mainly on Tuesdays so that the rotary system could carry on.

What happened? Sterioff, back at 155 College Street, squirmed when I asked. He's not in charge there anymore, and any principal must have the right to run his own school, he said. I told him Main Street had adopted a fairly rigid, traditional approach to schooling, that it didn't seem very culture oriented anymore, that the motivation was extrinsic, that it prepared pupils for high school rather than for life. All the agreement he would give was: "That could be."

To Sterioff, Main Street lives. He gave up the principalship in 1967 to spread its philosophy across the system as chief New Canadian consultant. But at Main Street, meanwhile, that inevitable metamorphosis back to conventionality gave the lie to brave theory. School there was better than many immigrants ever had it before, and perhaps better than they would ever have it again. But it was just school.

"I think we try to make our school as much like one of the high schools as we can . . ." teacher Marilyn Mulligan told me. "When I first came here in January of 1968, it was all very oral, we did more talking. That was the first six months, and then we got more written work into it. . . . I really feel we send the students far more equipped to enter high school."

"They told us, 'Your kids speak good English, but they can't write'," Andy Pandoff said in an unguarded aside after the slide show. This was one reason for the gradual change from strictly oral-aural, culture-based learning program. The message came from the high school principals and guidance counsellors, and the response was predictable. "So now we're offering a broader range of learning experiences; we offer reading and math and some science. The teachers still teach English, using these subjects as vehicles."

It was the spring of 1974 before the truth came out about how Main Street's graduates got treated once they left Main Street. Live-and-learn was all very well, but it meant these students became fodder for the system's vocational stream. Almost half of those who graduated into high school during its first two years — in 1966-67 — went vocational, and another third landed in the Big Techs or the commerce schools. A bare one fifth achieved collegiate status. As the program discarded its progressivism, the collegiates began to accept them. In 1972-73, 47 per cent went collegiate and only 6 per cent vocational.

One school in the system hardly could be expected to turn upside down the prerequisites of the secondary schools. It was naive to try to prepare for the tedium of high school by having "set pupils free to explore and discover the topography and inscapes of their community" as Sterioff's pamphlet had urged. To flood one small school — a New Canadian school at that — with progressivism was to offer the kids no real purchase on the school system. To complicate it further, Main Street not only was not typical of Toronto schools; it certainly wasn't typical of Italian, Greek or Portuguese schools. For some pupils, this easygoing, laissez-faire program required a double adjustment: first to Main Street, then to a regular hard school. "In Main Street you play a lot," one Grade 9 graduate said. "You don't have to study like here...."[5]

Whatever it did to wreck the ideals of those visionaries who founded the program, the moderation of Main Street probably made entry into Toronto school life less traumatic

[5] "Main Street School and Regional Reception Centres: a comparison of graduates" by Susanne Mowat, Research Department, Toronto Board of Education, August 1969, p.31.

— if less truly educational — than it was before. The change came quietly under the tenure of George Baker, a reading-and-writing principal who followed Sterioff and then took over Dundas School. The glittering world of pilot projects is such that programs fade without notice once the spotlight shifts. The outer forms harden as the inner program reverts to conventionality, and scarcely a word can be found to document the change. Few were to know, much less care, that a dream died at Main Street.

In 1969, Susanne Mowat of the Research Department did a study of Main Street and reception centre pupils who were then in Grade 9. Their own assessment jarred the assumptions of the entire program. "There was only one issue — language, regardless of any philosophical positions their Canadian educators might have," she concluded. It was a slap on the face to Sterioff visionaries who promulgated culture as the vehicle to speech. But to this researcher at least the verdict was clear: "In fact, the implication of some of the students' statements, if one wishes to draw it, might be that they have a different philosophy: one of learning the language which they identify as vocabulary and pronunciation, as efficiently as possible, and letting cultural integration follow that."

Once they can speak and write English, they are not helpless. They can work, they can earn money, they can buy security. Until they learn English they are the easy victims of their new society, unable to fend for themselves against its economic and cultural incursions. English is what they all said they needed first, partly no doubt because the larger school system itself made language competency a key to success. But by pushing culture before language, New Canadianism was opting for assimilation as a prerequisite of personal power.

Main Street School was but one lighthouse along the

coast of New Canadian programs.[6] Under Sterioff its philosophy became the guiding light throughout. But in the west end the arrivals were heavier, allowing reception centres at each school. And Kenneth Fisher, a teacher at King Edward School, kept alive the notion of language training and native identity in the face of Sterioff's cultural approach.

There were, in all, reception centres, withdrawal programs and transition classes for nearly 6,000 students; there were summer school and evening classes for 3,000 children and 7,300 adults; the cost of all the New Canadian services was liberally estimated at $4-million a year in 1972, about 5 per cent of the operating budget.

This includes a corps of interpreter-counsellors, social workers and psychologists who boast "a combined proficiency in 42 different languages" according to one Board of Education fact sheet. It also includes the translating of brochures into the native tongues. One example is a publication on venereal disease, put out in separate two-colour editions in Chinese, Greek, Italian, Polish, Portuguese and English. The Board of Education's commitment to immigrants is no mere tokenism; it is substantial. Is it what's needed?

Along St. Clair Avenue West stands a 58-year-old schoolhouse that does not belong to the Toronto Board of Education. It is a Catholic school, run by the Metro Separate School Board, and host to 950 elementary school kids, all but 100 of them Italian. I went in a side door off Northcliffe, through a wooden lobby, up an open staircase, past an elevated alcove, and into a narrow, wood-paneled hallway with coathooks and backless benches along both walls,

---

[6] In September 1974 it had to move to Greenwood Secondary School, because a repair job to make the stairwells fire proof would have cost the board $300,000.

and a low-slung sink with two large water taps at one end. The other end led into a classroom. Here is where Silvana Toscano conducted her class of 12 immigrant children in the most natural way possible — in both Italian and English.

The place had a touch of mustiness, the smell of aging varnished wood. High windows looked out on the Catholic church with arched windows and a little white cross. The inside wall had windows, too, high above the slate chalkboards, opening onto the hallway. They were neatly encased in hardwood with square blocks mortised into the corners: the place had not been mass produced; it was built to endure. A crucifix hung high on the north wall; beside it were prayers in Italian and English.

Here Toscano did her thing. Her talk, gutsy and direct, was a formidable mixture of languages. All her Italian charms came to life with the lesson at hand — flourishes, frowns, laughs, gentle ridicule, harsh commands, nudges and caresses. She talked because she had something exciting to tell, no twinges of condescension. "Oh come on, don't be silly," she told a curly haired boy who insisted she stick to Italian.

Their religion class came first on Monday mornings. Fittingly, the lesson was about St Francis of Assisi (1182-1226) who inspired St Clare, a good woman of Assisi, Italy, to start the Second Order of St Francis, an order of nuns that followed all the Franciscan rules of poverty except one, going out to beg. Their Italian text, *Studiamo insieme,* was published in Milan. It mingled religion, history, geography, grammar, mathematics, geometry, and biology into one diversified whole. Not old fashioned at all, Toscano assured me. She had a brother teaching in Italy who kept her posted on the latest trends. This was one of the best. Beside it, their English text, *Magic and Make Believe*, seemed bland pasta, but they labored through both of them under Mrs Toscano's choreography.

St Francis was supposed to be studied in Italian, but Toscano threw in an English sentence now and again to push them. Salvadore, who immigrated that August, objected, "This is Italian," he told her in Italian. "I want to stick to Italian, I don't want to hear any English."

"All right then," she laughed, "We'll speak Italian." Which they did. "I don't blame Salvadore for that," she told me later, "He's Italian and he's very proud."

Later they were practicing a play in English when Salvadore answered a question in Italian. She flared at him. "You said we'd do Italian when we're doing Italian, and English when we're doing English. Well now we're doing English." And he did.

Toscano herself came from Calabria eleven years ago. She had been teaching in Toronto for seven years, always strictly in English because that was what the superintendents required. "When I taught them the old way," she recalled, "I couldn't use any Italian, and it was heavy. Very heavy. Now I teach them ordinary subjects while I concentrate on the English. They are convinced in their own minds they must learn English; it's just a matter of doing it gradually."

Her cross-cultural liberties allow the kind of tie-ins that could scarcely happen in an all-English setting. The class was reading *Magic and Make Believe*; they ran into a "Mr Brown" and started sniggering. "Some Italian names are funny, too," she told them. "And Italian names have colours. What about rosso? That would be Mr Red."

A child shouted, "Mr Marrone." Laughter.

"All right," she said, "we don't have Mr Marrone. Maybe Italians don't like brown, but we do have funny names, too."

Her familiarity with Italy also let her know the special problems of learning English. For example, Rugo pronounced his "d's" like "t's" because, Toscano explained, his own Italian dialect was that way. He came from the town of Bari near the Adriatic Sea. She drilled him on his "d's".

Nicola, she pointed out, is exceptionally bright. His English was already quite good. In Italy he got 9's and 10's, which is tops. "If that child were in a classroom with only English, he wouldn't feel the same," his teacher told me. "He would feel less than he was before."

This isolated escape from the rigors of New Canadianism was brought about by Kent Henderson, an associate professor of psychology at the Ontario Institute for Studies in Education, a sandy-haired, diffident man. He settled on St Clare School after the Toronto public school trustees turned him aside and North York trustees could not find enough new immigrants. The Catholic trustees were only too glad; so was Toscano, who always wanted to teach that way anyhow.[7]

What he set out to do was to teach newly arrived Italian youths their ordinary school subjects in Italian, while giving them strong doses of English language training. This would keep them abreast in their studies until they had learned enough English to merge with their peers.

It was hardly a revolutionary idea, only in Ontario it was new. And it had some good logic behind it.

Already in 1962, the Research Department put out a report suggesting that schools should try to preserve native languages. Children quickly lose their powers in a first language after switching to a second; the report pointed out that a child's inability to speak his parent's language often intensifies family conflict. A point not lost to the researchers was that the schools themselves might benefit in the

---

[7] The Metro Separate School Board always has been inclined to favor ethnic concerns. Its trustees are chiefly Irish and Italian; it also has three elementary schools in Toronto for French-speaking children.

goodwill created by preservation of the mother tongue.

A few years later, evidence started rolling in that showed children do best in English who learn to read and write their native tongue first. Nancy Modiana did her Maya highlands study in 1966, showing that children first taught to read in their native Tzeltal and Tzotzil did better in Spanish than those taught only Spanish. This set the stage for many more to follow, which were finally assembled and reviewed by the Research Department in January 1974.

The Henderson approach was partly a reaction to the rigor of New Canadianism, and partly a return to common sense. In Toronto's highly streamed system, at the critical age of 12, a year lost could throw a child into a two-year high school — or worse, into a vocational school — dashing his hopes for a trade or university. And immigrant parents, themselves ignorant of the system, would not know the real consequences until long after the fact.

"Behind the creation of our study," Henderson told me, "is principally the report that a lot of immigrant students are streamed into the terminal, rather than the academic, high school stream." I thought it was damning stuff if true, and I spent a lot of time sifting the evidence from the Board's own statistical studies. Henderson had commented on the obvious outcome of that sort of placement. "If you get streamed into the terminal stream, it's fairly difficult to get reinstated in the academic stream. . . . It can be done, but it's easier to go down than up."

Henderson's assumption about the downward streaming of immigrant children has a shred of truth. The facts do show that a higher proportion of non-English immigrants end up in terminal schools than do native Canadians. The figures are roughly 20 per cent of immigrants, 15 per cent of non-immigrants.[8] But this comparison is not what it seems;

[8] "Students' Background and its Relationship to Class and Programme in

these statistics used alone ignore one important variable: socio-economic class. The pertinent fact is that immigrant parents are twice as likely to be in the lower socio-economic bracket than non-immigrant parents.[9]

If this is taken into account, immigrant children are no more or less slighted than their lower-class Canadian peers. It turns out, though, that Henderson's assumption is valid for the particular children he attempted to help. They had the misfortune of immigrating at a time of life when the Great Divide in Toronto would soon stream them almost incontrovertibly toward their station in life. As immigrants, they would not have time to learn English and recoup the lost year of academic learning before the Grade 8 sort-out.

On the whole, however, immigrants do share the lot of their neighbours in the inner-city communities of Toronto. As members of the lower working class, they are held in place by the social institutions around them, not least the school. It is cruel myth to assume that immigrants fall into the lower streams for lack of family motivation. As Kurt Danziger showed in a 1971 study,[10] Italian immigrant families in Toronto are at least as eager for academic success as are native Canadians. Far from forcing their children to drop out, they often promote unrealistically high aspirations. Unrealistic, that is, for the institutions in which they must succeed. He says it is the students themselves who realistically trim their ambitions when they realize the cards are stacked against success.

Henderson would make no dramatic claims for the St

School (The Every Student Survey)" by Edgar Wright, Research Department, Toronto Board of Education, Dec. 1970, p.28.

[9] "Parents' Occupations, Students' Mother Tongue and Immigrant Status: Further Analyses of the Every-Student Survey Data" by Edgar Wright and D.B. McLeod, Research Department, Toronto Board of Education, Sept. 1971, p.4.

[10] "The Socialization of Immigrant Chidren," Part 1, by Kurt Danziger, Ethnic Research Program, Institute for Behavioural Research, York University, Oct. 1971. p.80.

Clare School experiment. The tests he did after the first year showed no major academic gains or losses, compared to control groups. But the results showed a strong likelihood his students would be just as bilingual in two years as their New Canadian peers, and just possibly more healthily integrated. He believes his approach less traumatic, its unmeasurable effects less drastic. "Sure," he says by way of analogy, "you can recover from an illness, but it might not have been necessary to be sick in the first place."

How much it hurts a child to have his own language ignored in a class of strangers probably never will be measured by the social scientists. They are interested in comparison, in results, in hard facts. Their quantitative devices measure only the costs and benefits as related to the political structure of the schools. You cannot measure feeling, you cannot quantify distress and fear. Talk about hurting children seems oddly archaic in the modern school setting that is geared to painlessness and enlightenment; it is something, like sex and petty theft, to be taken quietly for granted. Yet, slowly, strangely, the elements that count for nothing in the grand designs of the system take their toll until somebody finds the sensitivity and courage to speak out.

The first crack in the armour of New Canadianism came with Anthony Grande's humble plan in April 1972 to have Italian youngsters learn both Italian and English at Toronto public schools.

Grande himself had arrived from Italy at age 11; he now taught at Earlscourt Public School. He was an ardent, soft-spoken man, tactful enough at the outset to push bilingualism more for its sound pedagogy than for its cultural, emotional or intellectual benefits to Italian children. "The primary objective," he said in an Action Profile, "is to help the ethnic child learn to read and write in English to the best of his ability. . . . These children have linguistic and cultural experiences which, if properly utilized, can work to the child's advantage and hence facilitate the introduction of the English language. The basic principle inherent in this approach is that the school begins *where the child is.* . . ."

But the human force behind this pedagogy had to do with the distress of small children. It takes little imagination to sense the damage to a child's self-esteem at having his culture and language totally ignored at school. A 5-year-old child is not a blank slate; Grande tried to stand up for the worth of a child's preschool acculturation. "What the schools do," he told me, "is what I call negative reinforcement. The schools, the teachers, the other social forces, they promote a negative attitude in the child toward his native culture. They may not want to produce that effect, but they do it simply by saying, 'Here we speak English'. The child in time will learn that forgetting Italian is the other side of learning English. He comes to despise his own origin."

All Grande wanted was a pilot project — one teacher and an assistant with 40 Italian kindergarten pupils — to start learning in Italian and gradually shift to English, until by Grade 8 the pupils would be equally bilingual. The cost would be $1,000 a year.[11] He reasoned that they could learn to read and write English better once they could read and write Italian, and that this attention to mother tongue would greatly improve the relationship between home and school.[12]

When Grande first made his proposal in April, the New

[11] This did not seem an outrageous price. That same year the board set up an entire school at the behest of a well-organized, middle-class group of academics. It was called ALPHA, and it cost over $100,000 the first year. The teachers were supplied by the board.
[12] Both of these points have been subsequently validated in the Research Department's publication, *Second Language Programs for Young Children,* by Stan Shapson and Mary Purbhoo, Toronto Board of Education, January, 1974.

Canadian Committee went apoplectic. Not until a year later was the Board to receive Grande's proposal, and then in sharply modified form. The committee, meanwhile, chose to seek clarification by the Minister of Education of the Schools Administration Act which appeared on the face of it to allow instruction in a third language only with the special consent of the Minister. It said:

> It is the duty of a teacher in instruction and all communications with the pupils in regard to discipline and the management of the school, to use the English (or French) language except where it is impractical to do so by reason of the pupil not understanding English, and except in respect of instruction in a language other than English when such other language is being taught as one of the subjects in the course of study.

Thus began a two-year hassle between school board and Ministry over how much leeway to allow, when and where to give in, and how not to give in. What eventually came out of it was a token program allowing Italian kindergarten children to talk Italian — but not learn to read or write it — at General Mercer Public School.

Thirty-five Greek parents crowded to the front of the Board Chamber on March 23, 1973, children scampering about, mothers shushing them, fathers looking serious like the solid working-class people they were. They wanted one hour a day of Greek instruction at Frankland and Jackman schools to keep their language alive. The board again foundered over what the Ministry would tolerate, and finally agreed to put it off six weeks until Director Ronald Jones had time to clear things up with the Minister. Then the board moved into a spirited 30 minute debate on whether to allow smoking at board meetings, which was, as trustee Fiona Nelson declared, "a very serious infringement on people's right to breathe." Smoking lost on a tie vote.

I called the Ministry after that meeting to find out its position; I found it without clear policy, except to unbend as little as necessary to avoid confrontation. D.A. Penney, chairman of curriculum guidelines, said the Greek proposal "would be a difficult request for the Ministry to accede to at the present time. . . . It's a question of seeing the school as the institution for achieving social cohesion as over against seeing it as the agency for personal fulfillment as the ethnic groups desire."

An amiable saw-off with ethnic groups had been reached; any brash confrontation was to be avoided. The Ministry would allow transitional bilingual classes at elementary schools and language course options at secondary schools. He described the problem to me as a matter of balance, weighing the need for achieving social cohesion against the desire for self fulfillment. This meant, of course, that students would be allowed to forget Italian in Grade 1 and then get a chance to learn Italian again in Grade 9. The irony did not escape him, but like the good civil servant he was, he would express no personal feelings.

The Board meeting in May had both the Grande proposal and the Greeks' proposal before it, and once more the debate hinged on what the Minister would allow, rather than on what the Board wanted. Trustee Barr tried to press Solicitor Douglas Gilmour to say whether both of the Italian proposals — Grande's original and the modified plan — couldn't be put before the Minister. Gilmour replied: "It is my opinion that the only purpose for native language to be used is for facilitating the pupil to absorb English." Barr said that wasn't his question. "It's simply my opinion that the Grande proposal would not be acceptable," the solicitor went on.

The Greeks were led by William Ainis, a gruff-voiced man who identified himself as a member of the Greek Parents' Association. "We're here today to demand our rights as Canadians," he said, reading from a yellow paper. "Our problem is that we cannot communicate with our children. We speak Greek and they speak English . . . If you really care about the Greeks of Canada, you will be agreeing to our demands."

Trustee Charlotte Maher of Ward 10 arose, rubbing her hands. The Greeks should understand that what they wanted was a privilege, not a right, she began. "Now I have a lot of respect for the Greeks, the Russians, the Chinese . . . but in no way can we offer you this program in our schools." Trustee K. Dock Yip didn't see why the Greeks wanted a whole hour a day. "One hour is too long. Twenty minutes." Ainis replied: "Twenty minutes is not long enough. One hour."

And so it went, until Mitchell Lennox, superintendent of the program, informed them the Ministry would agree to the program as long as it dealt with cultural aspects of Greece and ran no more than 30 minutes a day. It should be "dwelling in the cultural, but not teaching language as such," he said. Douglas Barr asked if one could read between the lines that "we can have language if it's disguised as cultural study." Lennox nodded.

"Then why not?" Barr said.

And so the Board unanimously, clause by clause, approved the Greek program as amended, and the Greek parents who understood little English caught the happy mood and clapped every time a clause passed, thinking they were getting what they wanted. A full year later, in the spring of 1974, they still had nothing. It was promised for that fall, provided the Greeks could supply their own staff.

It became clear that the establishment had got the word. Remaining steadfast, the officials weren't going to put a proposal forward that the Minister would have to reject. By this time the board had been cajoled by its officials into asking the Ministry in advance, rather than deciding and then confronting the Ministry, so there was little more they could do. The trustees threw a futile motion to the Grande original — it lost 4-13 — then unanimously approved what the Minister of Education had said he would allow.

It would be a withdrawal program, 30 minutes a day, staffed entirely by volunteers, at no cost to the Board of Education. The Canadian culture was well as the Greek was to be studied, and the parents were to be involved in the school. What the Ministry allowed them wasn't very much, hardly a resemblance of what they had requested, but in the hands of the New Canadian experts it soon took on a marvelous new image. "This is a quantum jump," Lafountaine had told the trustees. "It's like a discovery of raw power. There's unlimited energy in the community; there's no such thing as entropy."

With these words stirring their blood, trustees approved what must be the wordiest proposal ever passed with so little substance to it. No offer of financial help, no offer of teacher time, no program of language training, no assurance that it would happen during regular school hours (this was, however, assured later). Lafountaine told the New Canadian Committee: "This is not a language program in any sense of the term. It is strictly a bicultural immersion program, and that involves the use of the language of the culture as well, but when we asked the parents what they wanted, we discovered they wanted cultural preservation." By turning this mind-bending logic on the Greeks and, later, the Chinese, the New Canadianists were able to redefine the need, and in so doing make it possible for the system to provide it.

The Greeks were given to understand they didn't really want just *language* preservation; they wanted *cultural* preservation. And getting something so much more glorious than they wanted, who were they to refuse? So the system gave them the icing but not the cake. The kids would grow up forgetting their native speech, not learning how to read and write it, but they would have all the cultural accoutrements, the dances, the games, the geography lessons.

The official name for it, the Bicultural-Bilingual Immersion Program, was a pompous bit of jargon. Immersion, as used in Toronto, implies being steeped in one culture for extended periods of time, as in the French immersion kindergartens. To be "immersed" in two cultures at once is to be immersed in none. The euphemism was nothing but a gimmick for getting a bureaucratically acceptable program past the parents on one hand and the Ministry on the other. The Greek withdrawal classes themselves were to be bicultural. "Expected to maintain," the Board's proposal said, "a reasonable 'Canadian' environment component in both the activity and the material." Yet despite the false advertising, the programs could be — as the Greeks and Chinese hoped — better than nothing.

The catch-word for Canadian culture is "mosaic", but the reality of Toronto's education system to this date is "melting pot".

Ontario's late-blooming immigration challenged its educators to react in a uniquely Canadian fashion. They chose New Canadianism. It turned out to be unique more in appearance than substance, for its progressive aims disguised the crassness of cultural assimilation. The Sterioff approach provided a way out of the negligence of the past without basically challenging the Anglo-Saxon supremacy upon which it was built. Until 1972, there was little criticism of his approach, and the popular press heralded Main Street's story as good news: "An old Toronto school with a brand new look is teaching 72 youngsters from all over the world how to be Canadians," the *Toronto Telegram* said in 1965. "There's a school in Toronto's east end that is turning out Instant Canadians," the *Star Weekly* announced. "A host of exciting activities designed to engulf and intrigue the children are used to make communication — in the English language — a necessity," the *Christian Science Monitor* chorused.

An implicit assumption of New Canadianism is that our social fabric is too fragile to withstand the onslaught of multiple cultures. This guise of vulnerability covers a flinty cultural chauvinism with which the educational and political elites direct public institutions. Into this same defence play all the fears for national survival, including ironically the very threat of American cultural takeover. Tight social cohesion is assumed to provide the Spartan strength to counter cultural subversion from without, yet sadly this very posture is the Americanism we abhor.

Researchers at Toronto's Bureau of Municipal Research once had the temerity to suggest that Canada is more receptive to the idea of a multi-cultural mosaic than is the United States, since from its beginning Canada has been officially bicultural. Logical it is, but not inevitable. It depends what Canadians will make of their own heritage, and the educational stance in this city has not been reassuring. Quite the contrary, Canada's own bicultural origin becomes the basis for multi-cultural fears, as if the federation of this French-English nation state could not bear the added burden of competing cultures. The peculiar Canadian anemia infects the system out of lingering guilt around the very bilingual fact with which Canada was born, so that what could serve as a liberating matrix has become repressive conformity.

Sociologists foresee Toronto moving toward a multi-cultural mosaic with the awakening and self-assertion of minority cultures. Anthony Richmond, a York University professor of sociology, sums up the movement and the tension: "The opportunity and desire to pass on a non-English language and cultural heritage may be much greater in the future than in the past, particularly if current federal and provincial government policies with regard to multiple-culturalism are successful, in the face of evidently strong economic and social pressures toward English language assimilation."[13]

Yet as it happens this trend toward cultural pluralism is a movement for which the Toronto school system can take no credit. Its vaunted New Canadian program has turned cultural awareness and ethnic pride into liabilities rather than sources of strength. "A true mosaic culture," psychologist Karl Furr noted, "would have to encourage the development of the language, culture, and talents of the many ethnic groups as well as give them the skills needed to survive as equals within the dominant English-speaking community." Advice not heeded. The fact that multiple cultures in Toronto are alive is a tribute to their own resilience rather than to the system with which they co-exist.

---

[13] "Multiculturalism in Toronto," *B.M.R. Comment,* Bureau of Municipal Research, 1972, p.6.

Chapter 3

A HIGH SCHOOL EPISODE

This chapter is a story from the underside of schooling, about how a probing insight thrown carelessly at the system triggered its bureaucratic defenses, how something good was salvaged at the end, and how it all happened on a stage set by distant governmental priorities. As an episode in one part of the city's highly differentiated system, it in no way suffices as an analysis of secondary schooling — for which this book is too brief. But it provides some clues.

One July evening, when the Last Great Exposé still lay safely under wraps, I met Marilyn Miller at the Maxwell's Plum in Yorkville. She was not the Amazon hearsay made her out to be. A shy, friendly sort, she had graduated from McGill University with a social work degree, and taken a job as attendance counsellor here two years before. At the moment, her main worry was selling her Renault so she could sail for England, where she had herself a job with the Jewish Family Agency of London. But she wasn't leaving very many friends behind.

West Park Vocational School. She talked about it warily. A lawyer had told her not to say anything. Any teacher "whose professional reputation or career is damaged by this smear" could sue her for libel; the Ontario Secondary School Teachers' Federation had promised to pay the

A High School Episode

teacher's legal costs. The school trustees themselves had not yet allowed themselves to read the things she had written.

What had Marilyn Miller done? She had co-authored a 33-page report on conditions at West Park Vocational School. "We wrote it," she told me, "because we were concerned, and these kids were getting screwed, and maybe in the vague hope that something would be done about it. We hardly expected this."

And what was West Park, but a newish brick building stout as a bunker, located on the southeast corner of Bloor Street and Dundas West, three minutes by foot from the subway, a seven minute run from High Park. The building was square and trim, four stories high, its central core containing a double gymnasium, a swimming pool, a 600-seat auditorium. Two dozen classrooms, three dozen shops. It had a bakery shop, a room full of 17 electric organs, a greenhouse, an upholstery shop, an electronic reading lab, a hair-styling salon, a mechanics garage, a limited-vision classroom, a hard-of-hearing classroom, drafting rooms and photography labs, cabinet shops and auto shops, a landscape area and a trowel trades centre, leather work and tailoring shops, a laundry and dry-cleaning place.

It had everything a youngster with limited occupational goals could ask.

Yet somehow or other, in the five years West Park was open, it had never been full. There was space for 932 students, but not more than 773 were willing to attend it at any one time, and thereby hangs a heavy tale. Something strange was happening behind that red brick exterior, and whatever it was, it seemed to keep students at bay. Parents weren't sending their kids to West Park if they could help it.

Was West Park, as Marilyn Miller had put it, becoming "a phantom school"? No more so than the four other vocational schools newly built as havens for the unfortunates of public schooling. If the schools were so fine, why were they getting empty?

So much had gone into them. Their modern expansion had begun in John Diefenbaker's Cabinet, where Labour Minister Michael Starr broached the topic of massive federal aid to technical schooling back in 1959. The prime objective was to move the nation out of a post-Korean War slump, in which unemployment ran a dismal 7 per cent, while skilled workers were in short supply. Starr hoped to replenish skilled workers in the long run, and create building jobs in the short run. His tool was the Technical and Vocational Training Assistance Act of 1960. It passed the Legislature without debate.

Ontario was ready. "Frankly, I look at this as a heaven-sent opportunity to get some of those things done," Premier John Robarts told his Legislature, and to round out the federal offer of 75 per cent grants to new technical schools, Ontario threw in 25 per cent, relieving local boards of the entire cost. By the end of it, Ontario had gobbled up more of the federal money than the other nine provinces and two territories put together, a rich 65 per cent of the total, roughly $450-million by the end of the decade.

Robarts filled these schools by instituting a new vocational-technical emphasis, splitting the high school curriculum into one academic and two vocational streams. The Robarts Plan pushed vocational-technical enrolment up from 35 to 43 per cent from 1963 to 1970, and pushed total high school retention up from 70 to 80 per cent. The school system, he said, must not only prepare students "for a happy and contented life in our society, but also, we must educate them to fill the needs in industry as it develops."

Ironically, local educators in Toronto were having contrary thoughts. The Advisory Council of the Metro School

A HIGH SCHOOL EPISODE

Board, a group of top-flight educators including executive director William McCordic, put out a report in 1959 urging that slow learners be kept in ordinary schools. It was not good for slow learners to be segregated, they warned. A diversified school environment was far better training for a diversified society, especially considering the fact that 93 per cent did not make use of their trade skills anyway once they got out. And it was also less expensive to keep these children in ordinary schools.

The sandstorm rising on the federal-provincial horizon soon submerged this local wisdom in acres of bright new facilities. The outcome in Ontario was 275 vocational-technical facilities, including West Park Vocational. Admittedly, many of the facilities were built into comprehensive secondary schools, and they were not just for the under-achieving child but for technical or commercial majors, and they provided a great boon to a diversified school system in Ontario. But in Toronto's uniquely segregated system, the big money went mainly into vocational schooling.

In short, local school authorities outdid themselves under the influence of federal monies, in the hope of making vocational education a prestige item in the educational supermarket. But for all that, the students felt edgy about attending these glamorous new facilities. "The students feel the name 'vocational' works a hardship, in that it imputes a sort of second class stature to the students in attendance," West Park student David Lewis told the Board in a letter. The Board obliged, and West Park Vocational became West Park Secondary. One by one, the other four vocational schools followed suit.

The late principal James Eckel of West Park, who began teaching at Toronto's very first vocational school in 1937, told me about the previous name changes. "We changed the name of that school three times while I was there," he said, "from Junior Vocational to Jarvis School for Boys to

Jarvis Vocational School — just to fool the public."

It never worked. No matter how splendid, vocational schools still had the aura of dead-end schools. That was where you went if the only other alternatives were to stay in Grade 8 or drop out. You came to West Park if the standardized tests put your IQ in the 50-75 bracket, you were multi-handicapped, behaviorally unmanageable, or simply slow. One physical education teacher, who took a $1,200 salary cut just to leave what was formerly called Parkway Vocational for a lower position at Jarvis Collegiate, described the social stigma this way: "Kids at Parkview Secondary (its new name) are really down on themselves. And the worst abuse they can hurl at each other is, 'You're a Parkview kid.' Nobody I ever knew at Parkview would ever tell their dates they went to Parkview, because immediately they'd think they were dummies.

"And interestingly enough," he went on, "it isn't just among the students. I also felt the same thing when I went to staff meetings where there was a cross-section of all the high schools and collegiates. Whenever I said something, it wasn't important because of where I was from."

Those who attended vocational schools from the very beginning were seen to be "a burden to the whole community unless trained to become socially adjusted and self-supporting citizens," Eckel had written in a history of Jarvis Vocational. Then as now, vocational schools served mainly the poor, and it was either educate them or have "potential delinquents roaming the streets of Toronto." Visions like these, as well as humanitarian motives, drove the system to provide schooling for the slow and impaired in such a way as not to impede the swift.

Thus vocational schools formed the lowest tier in Toronto's many-layered high school system. Above them were the Level 3 high schools, formerly called the two-year schools. Above them were the commercial schools and the big technical schools. And above them in social ranking were the collegiates.

But vocational schools? Not even teachers really wanted to be there for long, except for the few dedicated souls devoted to the cause. When I asked Eckel why the staff reacted so sharply to the Miller criticism, he explained. "We had teachers who had worked themselves up academically to a point where they were expecting advancement . . . They were under the fear that this would be a dead end school for them, too."

In March 1972, Marilyn Miller told chief social worker John Boys what she had seen at West Park Vocational. He asked her to put it in writing, and novelist Joy Tepperman, working as a casework aide, helped her put together the 33-page document. Much of it was from a journal Marilyn Miller had kept during her 1½ years at West Park. The Miller-Tepperman report hung for eight months over the system before it broke, and by that time it was almost legendary. When it finally became public, it was remarkable not so much for its horror stories as for its tales of personal neglect and futility. West Park, the report said, "simply is not meeting the needs of its students." Then it scraped the thick underbelly of vocational schooling for all the examples anybody could want.

It was not a tightly written report. It rambled. But in a concerned, careful way, it gradually built into a full-scale indictment. Miller and Tepperman took up the cause of the misfits, the small fraction of vocational students who do not quietly conform. "They suffer from both cultural and emotional deprivation, and there is a genuine lack of parental support," they said. To these children, disrespect and squalor were all around, and the schools were just part of the squalid picture. For example:

> The poor opinion of themselves these students bring with them is only reinforced by the teachers at West Park Vocational. The teachers feel the students are dumb and won't learn anything, hence they don't . . . It is self-fulfilling prophecy. We have teachers at West Park Vocational who openly ridicule the students. One particularly vicious . . . teacher never misses an opportunity to embarrass and ridicule his students and has often referred to his students as a bunch of mental retards . . . . Time and time again, we hear cries of 'hey, stupid!' emanating from a teacher's mouth and filtering down the hall. Time and time again, when the social worker has gone to discuss a particular child with a teacher, the teacher has taken a particular delight in gleefully delineating the student's faults loud enough for the rest of the class to hear.

And so it went. They gave example after example, being very hard on the teachers. They said the good teachers that did come, didn't usually stay long because of lack of support "plus their own frustration at not seeing any positive results."

The report did not blithely blame the school while ignoring the home, or the effect of poverty and demoralization. There was Frank, who had been absent too much and acting up too often, and was referred to the social work department. Both parents, it turned out, were alcoholic. The father often beat up the mother. Frank coped by creating "his own phantasmagorial world where he was able to bolster his self-image sufficiently to survive." They had him tested at the Hospital for Sick Children, and found him to be "dangerously psychotic and schizophrenic."

There was Henry, who could neither read nor write. He got referred to social work for truancy. "His frustration was so great that when he was persuaded to return to school, his behavior was so belligerent and aggressive he invariably got into trouble with both the teachers and other students."

Children with this spread of problems clearly required exceptional teachers — "the kind of teacher West Park is definitely lacking," Miller and Tepperman declared. In fact, their report and its aftermath portrayed teachers as being exceptional in much the way the students were. They were seen as insecure, disturbed and sometimes brutal. One teacher balked when a case-aide offered a child reading help outside class for fear the child would then lose interest and skip class. Their criticism centred on the fact that many teachers lacked the sensitivity for the job, and that those who had it would soon move out.

The sensational aspect in the Miller-Tepperman report lay in its description of physical abuse. "Behavioral problems are dealt with by the teaching staff in a blunt, physical way ranging from a slap on the back of the neck with a ruler to being thrown against walls, lockers and doors, or simply beaten up. The social workers have often heard teachers brag of such incidents and have witnessed this physical abuse first hand."

Principal Eckel's reply was a total denial. Director Ronald Jones' reply was to say that the accounts of physical abuse were based — with one or two exceptions — on hearsay evidence. "There is no strap in the school," Jones wrote. "The principal has not strapped a student, nor authorized a strapping, since the Board of Education directed that corporal punishment not be used as a method of controlling behavior, and none has taken place in the school so far as he or the vice-principal is aware."

This was true. It had been almost a year since the strap had been outlawed by the Board, but Principal Eckel had not been a heavy strapper anyway. The record shows he allowed the punishment only seven times in 1969-70, always on the optional basis that a boy — he strapped no girls — could get off by going home and bringing his parents. The cause of the strappings? The strapping log lists the provocations: "Persistent disturbance of classes. Damage to school property. Indecent behavior." West Park had a mild record compared to the East End High School, later called Lakeview Secondary. It had 101 strappings in one year, and it was a Level 3 school. The only high schools that used the strap at all were those for children with IQs below 100, to put it in crude academic terms. The collegiates and tech schools never beat students — at least not officially.[1]

No doubt about it, the Miller-Tepperman report contained some errors. For example, it put the absentee rate at 36 per cent; Jones corrected this to 17 per cent, based on school records.

For all its mistakes, the report exposed the troubles of vocational schooling more graphically than they had ever been seen before. Which accounts for the trouble Marilyn Miller had in getting anybody who could do anything about it to read it. And that is a little story in itself, showing how things happen when the system sees itself to be under attack.

When John Boys did nothing with it, she took it to Gertrude Fatt, then superintendent of special services, with a copy to Education Director Jones. Jones took it to Solicitor Douglas Gilmour, who gave the verdict that "the report, in

---

[1] Getting strapped involved a pupil holding his hands flat open, and allowing the principal to whip them with a 16-inch-long, 1½-inch-wide, fabric-and-rubber strap. The practice had declined sharply during the 1960's, but when the board moved to stop it altogether in 1971, Jones pleaded not to have it legislated out. "If one legislates against a specific type of punishment," he told the board, "the alternatives adopted might be less helpful to the situation and sometimes more harmful to the individual psychologically." The West Park report gave unhappy evidence that Jones knew his system.

my opinion, is defamatory." He later warned the trustees not to look at it for fear of libel action, a threat the Ontario Secondary School Teachers' Federation backed up with an offer of legal aid. It did identify certain teachers, and it was libelous in certain parts. Those parts could easily have been deleted if the administrators had wanted trustees to know the basic criticisms of the report. But the administrators did not offer this, and the trustees did not request it.

By July 6, the reform trustees had forced the topic of the secret report onto the agenda. An angry debate resulted in nothing but a promise by Jones to look into it and report back, which he did five months later. The trustees voted 3-15 not to see the report, not even in a private meeting. "We are held responsible for the affairs of this school," Trustee Graham Scott had argued, "yet there are certain events about which we cannot even become aware." That was the way it was.

Jones' report the following December replied to eight major points, passed over a few others, and met the basic criticism with cool, noncommittal objectivity. "The report," said Jones, "is an emotionally written document" — a vice his own report could never be accused of — "with a number of highly inaccurate statements and unsupported statistics. Nonetheless, it points to several weaknesses in our present arrangements that should be examined and improved." The weaknesses Jones found to improve were reflected in his proposals. He wanted guidelines to define the role of the social workers. He wanted better communication. He felt somebody should work out better techniques for handling disruptive behavior. He wanted the board to review the purposes of vocational education and seek better teacher training programs. His proposals were invitations to ennui.

Inevitably, the Miller-Tepperman report came out. In

February 1973, I got a copy from the Community Schools Workshop and wrote a story for *The Globe and Mail*. We carried it on the front page along with a story from Principal Eckel, who denied all the criticisms. I also included Jones' disclaimers. Yet printing that story even with the disclaimers was like shaking a coconut tree. The countercharges fell so fast that vocational schooling soon became the big issue of 1973.

The big guns were out to discredit Marilyn Miller, who by this time was in London. "The people who wrote the report are as much on trial as the school," declared Trustee William Charlton, who wanted to pay her air fare to Toronto. OSSTF President Daryl Hodgins sent out denials to all media, and OSSTF Communications Officer Jack Hutton mapped out the counter-attack. The report, said Hodgins, "is a distorted document which seeks to divide a school staff from its students and community. In the process, it has seriously upset students who did not deserve to be upset. And it maliciously smears teachers whose professional reputations and careers ought not to balance upon one piece of atrocious and biased research."

Hutton was the writer for the then General Secretary Donald Felker's paid column in the *Globe*; he told Eckel in a letter: "I would like to demolish everything the *Globe* has been saying in the Teacher Views space this Saturday. This is exactly why the column exists, and exactly why we have laboured to produce a considerable audience so that we can speak up on occasions like this without fear of editing or censorship . . ."

Three days later, Felker's ghost-written Teacher Views appeared eight columns wide under the headline: *West Park Secondary School is one of the finest — anywhere*. What followed was a flat denial of the Miller-Tepperman charge that students at West Park are "thrown against walls, lockers and doors, or simply beaten up." One hundred West

Park students interviewed next day were reported to have said they didn't even recognize the school described by Miller and Tepperman.

The Hutton column informed the public that 27 per cent of West Park's teachers were fluent in a second language, that West Park had a champion midget soccer team two years running, that West Park had a Students' Council that planned activities such as a week-end camping trip that was videotaped by students, and that West Park provides special classes for those with impaired vision and hearing.

A few months later, the OSSTF hired Larry Collins, former *Toronto Telegram* writer, to do a brochure called *West Park Story*, and once more the school revealed its bright side. Its first article was entitled: "Image building to face an adult world."

After the report had been published in the newspapers, quoted on the radio and mentioned on television, the school trustees still thought better of reading it. But on February 6, 1973, when they again refused to read the report, they voted unanimously for a motion by Trustee Gordon Cressy to set up a work group of six trustees and two professionals to study Toronto's five vocational schools. That could have been the end, but Cressy made it the beginning. He handpicked the members and laid out the terms, and it was unlike any committee the system had seen before. For an outlay of $800, in less than eight weeks, it put together a major review of vocational schooling.

The group members sat through days and nights of closed and open meetings, talked to principals, teachers, students, caretakers and parents, visited a school in Ohio, spent time teaching at West Park, and then retreated to Aston Villa to draw together their analysis and proposals. Donald Rutledge, as head of the Language Study Centre, crafted their report; his expertise shines from the mimeographed pages, but the report also speaks of weeks of honest work.

The work group, in its research, had run into a wide range of reactions. Forty-five persons attended its West Park public hearing. Three of them were parents; most were teachers and administrators. "This is not a witch hunt or a fault-finding mission," Trustee Vernon Copeland began, pouring oil on troubled employees. The meeting skirted the issues like two lions circling for advantage, seldom daring to leap. For a long time nobody seemed able to ask a straight question. It went like this:

> Vice-principal: You said that you had heard that there are people and some teachers who state that there is not enough challenge in the academic programs, especially reading. Did I hear you say that?
> Trustee Vern Copeland: I would be more accurate if I was to say it was an unanimous student perception and this was also expressed by some teachers.
> Vice-principal: I challenge those words, and say that we are going to look into this further.
> Copeland: I think this is a matter we are going to have to give consideration. It just seems to be from our two levels so far.

It was institutional madness, but through it all one parent did get a chance to complain about the change of name: "It would tend to give a parent a misconception as to the type of education his child is getting." And a shop teacher got a chance to tell Trustee Dan Leckie, who questioned whether the school was providing answers to his questions: "I resent that remark. You're feeling paranoid, that's all." Another participant, a bakery shop instructor, got a chance to divulge the essence of a vocational education: "They learn to open a door for a lady. These things they don't

A High School Episode

know yet. We are trying to educate them to fit into some situation so they will be able to hold a job. This is number one. We have been teaching them a trade besides. This is an added benefit.''

Later, at a big meeting at 155 College Street, you had Fernando Feliz, vice-president of Parkview's student council, telling it like it was:

> The first thing I want to say is that in public school, before I went to Parkview Vocational School, I was given a block. And I was made to put little circles in circles and little triangles in triangles. And then they said to me, 'Well, you're dumb. So we're going to put you in a vocational school!' They didn't make it clear to my parents that I would be going to Parkway. They didn't say I had a choice of Parkway, Castle Frank, or any other high school. They said, 'you are going to go to this school because it is good for you.' So I went to this school. The first year it really was fantastic; I was taking shop, I was enjoying classes. The second year, it was all right. The third year comes: and I am doing the same thing that I did the second year and the first year . . . I am suggesting one solution. I wish that we had individual timetables in that school. So you can pick what you like and what you are interested in. And you're not made to feel that it is a prison, and you have to do things, or else you're a bad boy and you've got a big mouth. I can understand the passes at lunch, we've had some trouble. Well, that's all right, passes at lunch, what's wrong with that? But in the morning we are made to stand outside on the C Block and if we do, we have to have a pass saying you can go to the library. At Eastern Commerce and places like that, they don't have to wait outside, they can go into the school. What that makes me think is that, it is a vocational school, we are

supposed to be mentally retarded. If you go outside at lunch without a pass, maybe you are going to kick some old lady or something. That's what it is. It makes you feel, 'Now calm down, just calm down, you'll get a job stirring paint or washing cars.' No, that's auto-mechanics. I don't want to say too much because my principal is here.

Another presentation that night was George Martell's analysis of vocational therapy. He built the case that at vocational school, whatever the talk about job training, nothing equals the students' getting "a sense of security and hope, a feeling of personal integrity and worth." Martell's point was that the hope is false, because vocational schools undercut the basis for it. Teachers may well try to relieve a non-achiever's pain with a little affection, but to exalt this into a school program was tantamount to betrayal. "Indeed, what the vocational school asks of its teachers, in the final analysis, is to encourage students to seal their birthright as potentially conscious and creative persons in the society for a little less pain."

The Work Group's interim report accepted Martell's analysis. It observed that what had begun in the Diefenbaker vision as a means of getting more semi-skilled people into the work force had become — in recent years — "at least as much concerned with therapy as with efficiency." School became a haven preparing kids to accept a welfare existence and to learn to like it. Martell and the Work Group nailed this fatalism as system-inspired. Students who learned to be happy inside but could not function outside the school had been done a disservice. This model, the Work Group said, "has the defects of all paternalistic organizations. It can communicate to the students a deep sense of their own inadequacy by patronizing them, protecting them, denying them the right to become adult."

A High School Episode

Last February, I was visiting a vocational school. The principal took me into a music room where 14 boys sat at organs, noiselessly playing into headphones. They were learning to sight-read *On Top of Old Smoky*. The teacher had his best student come to the master organ in the centre of the room and do a rendition. Then the principal spotted Ernie, across the room. "I'd like to hear Ernie play. He's my favorite," the principal called. Turning to me, he muttered: "A real tough kid, that boy." Ernie didn't want to play *On Top of Old Smoky*, but since the principal and teacher both insisted on it, he finally began playing with his organ turned as low as possible. The principal reached under the organ with his foot and turned up the volume. "Well," said the teacher when it was finished, "he can do *something*."

"He's a good boy," chimed the principal.

"Yes, he is," the teacher said, turning sternly to Ernie, "and let's hope he *stays* that way."

One main Work Group proposal was to mix vocational students in with Level 3 students. Vocational schools, it should be understood, took only Level 1 and 2 children. This is the bottom strata in a system that divides academic work not just by grade, but by difficulty. It is an internal method of sorting children without the open scandal of grading.

There are six levels of difficulty. Level 1 is basic, Level 2 is developmental, Level 3 is practical, Level 4 is general, Level 5 is advanced and Level 6 is enriched. A child taking Grade 12 geography at Level 2 would be getting something equivalent to the old-fashioned Grade 5 geography. A student who takes Grade 12 geography at Level 6, on the other hand, is university bound. The level system is one of the finely graded mechanisms that makes Ontario's new high school credit system work. Nobody fails, he only gets streamed, and there is supposed to be no shame of failure in that: *everybody* gets streamed. A rule of thumb is that a Grade 11 child pulling marks of 80 in a Level 3 course would pull 60 in a Level 4 course and 50 in a Level 5 course. All this, in short, is a grading system within a grading system. A child in vocational school can finally get a Grade 12 diploma, just like somebody from Central Technical School can, only it won't be worth much to anyone who knows the credits were earned at Level 2.

Vocational schools, at any rate, were Level 1 and 2 until 1974. In old-fashioned terms this meant that they had intelligence quotients ranging from 50 to 75, as measured by the Gates-MacGinitie Intelligence Test, or a reading level below Grade 5. The Work Group's proposal to put them in with Level 3 students — at Bickford Park, Brockton and Castle Frank — did not make the principals of those schools happy. They turned out at the October 1973 hearing to warn about the vicissitudes of intermingling.

John Keleeg, principal of Castle Frank, used his experience at Jarvis Junior Vocational School, where students of various low mentalities did mingle in the past, as an object lesson. There had been Ron, a 220-pound slow mover — "we couldn't get him beyond Grade 4" — and then this other 15-year-old greaser "just cut this fellow up something fierce." And Mike, a blind child. Students with limited abilities had a lot of compassion for Mike, but there were a lot of senior students who didn't. Cliff was a fantastic swimmer, Keleeg recalled, his voice dropping to an intimate low. Cliff "related" well in vocational school, but one day he said: "Those girls in regular school always made me feel inferior." So that's how it probably was with lots of boys in co-educational schools, a trauma Keleeg wanted to save them from.

Pupil's inhumanity to pupil was Keleeg's rationale for keeping his school untainted by retards. The reason the

A High School Episode

slow could be hurt in ordinary classes was that the classes were too large, they were run on the basis of competition, or they had insecure teachers. The teaching staff at Castle Frank High School stated blankly that "the sophisticated Level 3's usually accept physically handicapped youngsters but they can be damaging to the mentally handicapped." But it was seen not as a challenge for confrontation and growth; rather as a static definition that had to be accommodated through continued isolation. By separating them, the schools cleverly hid the fact that the school system itself fosters the feelings it finds fundamental to its separations.

The unification of the two lowest streams was one small step toward a sensible system. The Board overruled the objections to start the new policy in September 1974: "Our study has convinced us that distinctions between Level 2 and Level 3 students are often arbitrary," the Work Group had concluded. "We further believe that the presence of Level 3 students will improve the public image of the schools and the student population's image of itself." Other changes brought by the Work Group were to make all the schools except Heydon Park, a girls' school, co-educational, to make Eastdale into a new kind of Collegiate Institute, to extend the work experiences of vocational students, and to reduce their isolation by setting up Local Advisory Councils of staff, parents, employers, local merchants, and senior students at each school.

Finally, they proposed transforming a vocational school from the "therapeutic" model to the "co-operative realities" model, in which the working place was to be the learning place, and the prime values were to be self-determination, awareness, cultural integrity and equality. Students would take work projects in the community; they would learn carpentry by starting a carpentry business.

They would go to school to work and come home with some hard-earned money. Its hope for success lay in local government; it would be controlled by students, parents, teachers and residents on a democratic model. The dream passed the board partly because "they didn't know what they were voting for," one proponent said later. Its development still lay tangled in the thick weeds of bureaucracy, but it was a little start.

The Work Group had the good grace to admit in its interim report: "the impetus for this Work Group came from the Miller-Tepperman report on West Park Secondary School . . ." Something hopeful had begun from those outrageous insights that Marilyn Miller jotted down in her journal, and then with the help of Joy Tepperman into that 33-page document.

Chapter 4

A LAST RESORT

"We don't think the kids in Opportunity Class are all that dumb. In fact, in their own neighborhoods, a lot of these kids seem pretty bright. How come people say they're so dumb at school?" These words came from Trefann Court, that hot-bed of creative desperation just across Shuter Street from Park Public School. They summed up the anguish of inner-city parents about the school system's program for slow learners.

It was just possible that school failure may not be all their fault, or even the fault of their children. This wild possibility surfaced briefly across the Continent, as the U.S. Headstart programs crumbled, the poor saw their dreams dismissed, and educators began to re-think the promises of schooling. A conference sponsored by the U.S. President's Committee on Mental Retardation raised the question of the "six-hour retardate" — the child who is retarded only at school. "Do these children become drop-outs," a report of the conference asked, "or pushouts from an often inflexible, irrelevant social system as reflected in their schools?"

Good question.

The Trefann Court Mothers, as they called themselves, were not the unwashed hordes their mention conjured up in the minds of bureaucrats. They were seven gutsy, down-to-earth women who couldn't stomach bureaucratic excuses. Among them, they had 43 children. "There was a time," said Phyliss Tomlinson, one of the mothers, "when we sent the kids to school and we thought, well, they're the Board of Education, they know what they're doing. But now we aren't so sure."

With the help of Wolf Erlichman, a Trefann Court community worker, this little group did a lot of studying and comparing. They made comparisons with nieces and nephews at places like upper-middle-class Deer Park School, and their own children were far behind. They began to suspect that the system had their children slotted just as society had them slotted. As James Lorimer described it, "They were being put in a category of 'slum kids' and 'culturally deprived' and this was sufficient to explain why so many of them couldn't read, had to go to Opportunity Classes, found themselves failing in the early grades, and ended up in dead-end technical courses at schools where they could receive no academic standing after four years work."[1]

The Trefann Court Mothers put together their brief in anger over a report put out by Graham Gore, director of education, and Norman Sweetman, associate director. "From our point of view," the Trefann Court Mothers declared, "the report is little better than a fairy tale." The Gore-Sweetman report had set out the conventional aims of special education, arguing that Opportunity Class was just what the name implied it was, by this definition:

> The entire program in an Opportunity Class is designed to provide each individual child with opportunities to experience academic success at his own achievement

[1] "The Mothers Who Wanted to Change the School System", *The Globe and Mail,* August 25, 1969, p.7.

level. With these feelings of success and the consequent improvement in self-image, come further opportunities to relate socially with other members of the group and to participate in meaningful and useful group activities.

Opportunity Class. The name was given to classes for slow learners in 1937. They began in Toronto as "auxilliary classes" in 1910.

According to Gore-Sweetman official version, these classes were wholly dedicated to the welfare of the handicapped. "The guiding principle has always been the desire to meet the exceptional needs of individual children," they wrote.

But according to *Centennial Story*, the school board's own history written in 1950, they had another function as well. Those first classes were set up to counter "the harmful effects of the presence of many mentally defective children." Such children were sorted out to allow the others to be taught unhindered, and on this rock, too, was built the city's system of special education.[2] It developed slowly until the 1960's, gathering humanitarian motives as it grew, until it burst out in 15 various types and levels, an elaborate array of services and expertise for children of all disabilities.

These "special" children were defined by their disabilities, and it was against this backdrop that children were taught to feel normal about themselves. To the conventional bureaucrat, this was sensible and convenient. Chil-

---

[2] The board's own official history, *Centennial Story* has this to say in praise of Robert Cowley, chief inspector from 1913 to 1926: "The inspector's greatest concern was the problem of subnormal children, who were scattered throughout the lower grades and who, in some localities especially, were so numerous and of such harmful influence as to make normal class work almost impossible. . . . Before his resignation in 1926, there were 44 separate classes established for mentally retarded children." Page 140.

dren came in groupings of types and problems. James Williamson, chief in special education, was talking about EMR's, and when I asked what that meant he said it was "educable mentally retarded". These were the slow learners, and he went on to say how the system is no longer giving labels to children as it once did. They are only told they have a "learning difficulty," and are withdrawn from ordinary classes to have it remedied. A fine thing, this lack of labels.

Even the bright have themselves joyously declared "exceptionally talented". They are provided for in richly varied and stimulating Saturday morning classes. Herbert Goldie, consultant for the gifted, bemoaned the fact that even the exceptionally bright regarded themselves as somewhat suspect. "I look at the gifted kids in the city, and they aren't proud of their intellects," he said. "That seems widespread in Canada. We would never get carried away with something intellectual the way we got carried away with Team Canada in the Russian playoff. Maybe it's just a matter of publicity. Maybe we don't promote it. But it somehow seems we're still in second gear. We can't get it into high."

The trouble with sorting out the bright, the slow, and the disabled is the things it makes of people. By focusing on these traits, it tears them from the wholeness of themselves as persons. With their exceptionality as handles, the system places them in settings where they will be treated as exceptions. This is a mechanistic view of human beings that suits the system more than it does the nature of human growth.

By the early 1970's, when the system of special ed had grown gigantic, research was showing that the setting up of separate classes served no useful academic function. We have it from research in Britain, according to Alfred Yates in *The Organization of Schooling*, that such selective procedures "not only contribute substantially to the sum of human misery but that they are also manifestly incapable of achieving the objectives for which they are intended."[3] And from the United States, in a major study by Walter Schafer and Carol Olexa that " . . . to the extent that the findings are valid and general . . . they suggest that, through the track system, the schools are partly causing many of the very problems of student alienation, rebellion, and failure they are trying to solve."[4]

It came not just from research, but from prestigious authorities, too. A National Study of Canadian Children with Emotional and Learning Disorders (CELDIC) reported in 1970: "We are convinced that the great disadvantage of special classes is the segregated status of both teachers and children within the school community, and the development by the child of a self-image of failure and inadequacy because of the stigma of this segregation. As though this were not enough, we also retain very serious doubts about the educational advantages of special classes."[5]

In Toronto, however, special education received its most powerful and effective challenge, not from academic researchers or dignitaries, but from the Trefann Court Mothers in 1969.

Psychologist Karl Furr told me it was the Trefann Court brief more than any other one thing that finally shook the system. "When the Trefann brief went through, there were several of us who said 'Yeah, there's a lot of merit in that.' A lot of the studies showed us there seemed to be no merit in having all these slow learners and behavioral kids in separate classes. A vast majority could manage very well with that extra bit of help on a withdrawal or counselling basis."

[3] Routledge & Kegan Paul Ltd., 1971, page 64.
[4] *Tracking and Opportunity, the Locking-Out Process and Beyond*, Chandler Publishing Co., 1971, page 71.
[5] *One Million Children*, page 115.

Opportunity Class was the largest category of special education, and to the Trefann Court Mothers it had been a cruel irony, a tool of discrimination in the guise of compensatory help.

Their brief assembled the facts, studies and arguments then at hand to back up their outrage as best they could. Evidence that has been disclosed since that time about Toronto schooling shows that in many cases they grossly understated the case. They said, for example, that suburban children were streamed into academic courses at three times the rate of downtown children. They also pointed out that people in the upper-middle class suburbia of Don Mills had a per capita income of $8,490, while in Cabbagetown it was $3,811. The disparity of placement also seemed to have to do with the disparity of income.

Their finding was innocently mild. Toronto's Every Student Survey of 1970 was to show in lavish detail how much the Trefann Court Mothers understated their case. Children of labourers were 24 times more likely to be placed in special classes for slow learners than were children of professionals. Labourers' children were 18 times more likely to end up in the dead-end Vocational Schools than their upper-middle class peers.[6] On the evidence the mothers had available to them, the conclusion seemed obvious. They wrote: "The school system directly discriminates against the poor. . . . If you think these figures don't indicate this, we want to know why."

Until this time, Opportunity Class had been conceived by school authorities as an undeserved blessing. It was the second mile the system was willing to go to compensate for the blight of poverty. Class sizes were reduced to 12 or 15 pupils per teacher, special learning aids were made avail-

---

[6] *Student's Background and Its Relationship to Class and Programme in School*, The Every Student Survey, by Edgar Wright, Toronto Board of Education, December 1970, pages 34 to 37.

able, a teacher's assistant provided. The Trefann Court brief bit the benefactor's hand. Learning had something to do with pride. The mothers were sure of it. And the school system had better be sure it wasn't promoting the problems it set out to solve. "Is the teacher really facing a child who can't learn," they asked, "or is she facing a child who doesn't want to learn from her in that setting and therefore *she* has a control problem which Opportunity Class solves?"

Another challenge had to do with placement. If Opportunity Class was only to be a last resort for severely handicapped children, as Sweetman and Gore implied, why were so many poor kids going there? "Further," the women asked, "if 'self-contained' Opportunity Classes are not considered a good idea for kids who are 'slightly below average' what about the whole system of 'self-contained' special education high schools?"

Special education was one place the establishment had outdone itself to meet the needs of its clients. By 1970 no major city in Canada had been more magnanimous than Toronto. The Hall-Dennis Report, *Living and Learning,* had cited Toronto's system as an example of "sophistication and variety". As the lengthy rebuttal was soon to tell the Trefann Court Mothers, "educators throughout North America consider the Board's program to be one of the best on the continent."

By the turn of the decade Opportunity Class was just one facet of the 15-sided jewel called special education. Opportunity Classes were for slow learners, encompassing roughly 2,600 children; their number had trebled in the previous decade. Excluding those in gifted classes and those in speech correction, this section alone accounted for 65 per cent of all the children in special education. The others were 280 perceptually handicapped, 110 behaviorally abnormal, 250 with health problems, 100 with language or reading trouble, 325 with hearing problems, 250 with physical handicaps, and 90 with poor vision. This multitude made up 9 per cent of Toronto's public school children, with 12 per cent of its public school teachers. On the face of it, the system had in no way shirked its duty to the handicapped and the maladjusted.

I found the well-to-do grateful. One mother living in Wychwood Park, a wealthy wooded community on the escarpment, was full of praise for the way school authorities had helped her perceptually handicapped eight-year-old. After testing and special tutoring at the Ontario Institute for Studies in Education, her boy was placed in a special class at Keele Street Public School at age 6. He got help from a perceptive teacher in a class of eight, and later entered the regular program. "The thing that impressed us," said the boy's father, "is that this whole apparatus of the school board — the psychologists, the social workers, teachers and principals — could all come to bear on the problems of one small boy."

A common middle-class explanation for the inner-city outcry was that the poor mistrusted special placement because it aggravated the feeling of being cut off from the mainstream of society. Edward McKeown, in an interview when he was chief inspector for special education, expressed this view: "Some people see special education as a plot to maintain the differences rather than as an effort to try to help the children who have differences."

On looking closely at the Every Student Survey, I discovered that special education itself helps the rich and the poor differently. The children of low-income parents were heavily represented in the ranks of the slow learners so-called the "educable retarded", while middle-class children dominated the new services, such as aphasic, limited vision, and dyslexic classes. The Every Student Survey shows that

11.2 per cent of all children with parents in the lower socio-economic brackets were in ordinary slow-learner and behavioral classes, while only 3.7 per cent of these children were in the new services. At the top end of the socio-economic scale, the situation was reversed: 2.4 per cent were in ordinary slow learner classes, while 5.7 per cent were in the new services. Whatever benefits the newer services of special education offered, the poor were not getting a fair crack at it.

It had been Edward McKeown's job to reply to the Trefann Court Mothers. A small, ambitious man with powerful glasses, McKeown prided himself in hard work and factuality. A visionary with a behaviorist bent, he came to education from business, and cut his teeth in central administration as an academic data processing coordinator. He computerized the board's attendance and grade reporting systems.

By his own admission, McKeown spent 2,300 hours during 10 months, mainly holidays and weekends, researching and writing the two major reports on special education. He turned out the first report, limited to Opportunity Classes, in the spring of 1970. He presented it one balmy June night to a full auditorium at Castle Frank High School. With all McKeown's time and that of his colleagues — this 60-page report had cost the system over $15,000 by McKeown's estimate — good money was not going to go down the drain by a wash-out reception. School officials rimmed the stage, McKeown at the far left, with all the trustees taking chairs to the right, and for every anticipated question, somebody had a reply. But the full house was mainly special educators — consultants, lay assistants, principals, teachers. The questions were tame, except for a few cracks by critic James Lorimer, who broke his poleaxe on McKeown's prickly statistics. The defense seemed ample.

The Trefann Court Mothers cowered at the rear, not

speaking. One of them, Noreen Gaudette, told me later: "It made me feel that there he was, stacked up there with all his brains, and what he knew was what other people had written. I'm not so smart, but I think I'm closer to the problem. If only he'd go out and see little people, instead of little figures, he'd know what he's talking about."[7]

Later, I visited McKeown in his sixth-floor cubicle at 155 College Street. He told me some of the rigors of his job, about the long hours he had spent writing those reports, about the psychotic mother who plagued his office almost daily about her son being placed in a class she didn't want. McKeown dealt with that case himself — along with all his report writing — and it troubled him a lot. But little of this came through in his reports. They were facts, figures and superlatives. His heavy-handed defense of the system obscured his sensitivity to human needs. Those 200 pages of factual data held 65 statistical charts, but no descriptions of classrooms, no names of teachers or parents, no emotion.

The second report, meanwhile, had been prompted by another unhappy scene. This was the infamous Brant Street School paddling affair. It appears that Robert Holmeshaw, a young principal at this little downtown school, took to paddling disturbed youngsters on the bum with an eight-ply laminated wood paddle. This was against board regulations; only strapping on the hand was permitted. Trustee Graham Scott retrieved the paddle from a teacher's desk drawer, bringing it to light at a management meeting where Holmeshaw obliged by telling just how and why he did it.

Education Director Ronald Jones strove for a civilized metaphor, calling it a "therapeutic reinforcement-type

---

[7] The Trefann Court Mothers shortly after took their children out of public school. On a shoe-string grant from the University of Toronto's Student Administrative Council, they hired two teachers, got themselves space at Dixon Hall, and started their own school for ten children.

therapy," while Holmeshaw called it an act of mercy.[8] The exposure drew such strong teacher protest that the board could do nothing but ask for another report. This time they wanted to know all about special education — not just Opportunity Class — and so McKeown began churning out facts and figures once more. Trustee Fiona Nelson alone had 58 questions, and McKeown's reply covered 145 pages.

What both the reports conveyed was perplexity at how such highly motivated service could be so thanklessly received. McKeown gave evidence nobody — not even the Trefann Court Mothers — would have thought to doubt, such as a passage extolling the excellence of the eleven consultants. "The combined strengths of personality, training and scholarship of this consultant group are unsurpassed anywhere else in North America." So there. He told how "the present two inspectors" — himself and James Williamson — were in such demand as panel members, media personalities, consultants and confidantes, that they hardly had the time. "The effort to maintain the high morale and esprit de corps of the teaching staff in the face of uninformed and unjustified attacks has been very demanding."[9] At the end of the report, the school officials had the spunk to ask that McKeown's own job be upgraded from inspector ($23,000) to associate superintendent ($27,000). This was not granted immediately; three years later McKeown got his reward as associate director ($36,000).

The reports reviewed all the salient facts. The teachers had a median experience of 8.9 years, and 79.8 per cent had taken at least one special course. The average class size is 15 pupils, compared to 32 in an ordinary elementary class. No child is placed in self-contained classes without Admission Board review and parental consent. Placements are re-

---

[8] "I didn't *strap* a kid in that class," Holmeshaw said, "because I didn't want to take that final step. I couldn't countenance it."

[9] A report to the Toronto Board of Education, February 18, 1971, page 29.

viewed annually. Eighty-five new classes had been opened in the previous five years for slow learners alone, but in keeping with new trends 15 pupil withdrawal programs had been started.

McKeown's report was statistically correct. The Trefann Court brief was emotionally true. The two reports came out of different worlds, one the highly professionalized sanctum of technocratic control, the other the fierce desperation of a community in distress. The McKeown reports ignored the socio-economic class factor: the Trefann Court brief accepted it as overwhelmingly evident. When I asked Mrs Gaudette if she read the McKeown report, she replied, "I read all I wanted from that report."

The Ministry of Education, meanwhile, was making its own attempt to tone down the presumptions of special education. Harry Fisher, then the Ministry's superintendent of special education, broke the word in a speech to the Ontario Educational Research Council in December 1970. He drew together the critical research to date and concluded that: "The weight of the evidence suggested that separated special programs produced little that is superior to what is produced in the regular class."

The admission came as a shocker to the guardians of special education. When Fisher made his speech, he drew an uproar of complaints. But the overall result was that special educators introduced a few more withdrawal classes, tried to shift more teachers into itinerant roles, and — mainly — changed their rhetoric. Now self-contained classes were only for the most *severely* handicapped. "Because a child is learning slowly doesn't mean he has to go to a self-contained class any more — that is dead," said Williamson. In precept, the system gave way to the new knowledge; in fact, self-contained classes remained.

Shannon Ferrier is a special education teacher at Park

School who takes pupils from ordinary classes for 40-minute doses of remedial reading. She says it works, even though it means the other teachers must take 37 to a class, in order to free up her time. "I had two Grade 7 boys who were reading at 3.3 (Grade level) at Christmas, and by the following fall they were at 6.5," she told me. Allan Price, her principal, believed this to be a great gain over the old Opportunity solution, which he said helped children become more socially adapted but didn't improve them academically. But his school still had three special classes for multi-problem children. "Obviously, some kids just couldn't take an ordinary class. There's one girl, she has a metal plate in her head and tubes in her ears. She's got physical problems, she's got emotional problems. It would almost be a travesty to put that girl in an ordinary class."

At the other end of things is Paul Osadchuk, a sincere, practical man of 25, in a little walled-off section of the otherwise open-plan Withrow Avenue Public School, alone with 16 special children. They are retarded, physically handicapped, troubled and troublesome. He does what he can.

"The attitude toward special ed kids by the teachers is what I would call primitive," he tells me. "Many of them label these kids as something they just can't do very much with. These kids have limited abilities and it's difficult to integrate them, especially when it's academically oriented. They need special skills and all that, and it's very difficult to integrate them."

He told me the regular classes would have to be much smaller if these children were to be included. Now they have 34, so it's out of the question. But the effect of lumping failures together is tragic.

"They consider themselves dummies. The other kids think of them as being all dingbats. And the kids themselves, when you try to integrate them into the ordinary classroom, they say, 'I'm too dumb, I can't do that work.'

"I don't ever recall anybody coming by to check out my

kids," he went on. "There's been no mention of that to me, about having my kids tested. In fact, I've requested it of the nurse. She said, 'Yes, your kids have been awfully neglected.' I don't know why it is. I guess it's that they've been categorized as 'special ed', and then they just don't think there's much more to do. They put them in here, and hope that the classroom teacher can do something with them."

McKeown declared in his reports that no child is left to stagnate in special education. Each child is reviewed once or twice a year, always in the hope of transfer out. But the careful procedures outlined at the top office seem less than careful out in the schools. Williamson told me each child has the combined attention of psychologist, psychiatrist, social worker, teacher and principal. An Admission Board sits for each child, and nobody is put anywhere in special education without parental consent.

But it is still the homeroom teacher who knows. The largest sortout occurs at the end of Grade 6. At that point pupils go either to the regular Grade 7, or to academic vocational. If they have stayed out of slow-learner classes, their chances are good. But the dividing line is the Grade 5 reading level. A child below that line at the end of Grade 6 will find himself slotted AV — academic vocation. He has one year there to boost himself above Grade 5. If he fails, he goes on to a Level 3 high school as a mere "transfer," rather than a "pass." From a Level 3 high school, he has no chance of university, and little chance of a trade. These schools have been dubbed "terminal" because they do not lead to university.

"How do they decide whether or not a child has passed?" I asked Marg Johnson, a Toronto school psychologist. "I have no idea," she replied. "I haven't been able to find any general answer to that. And it's not because I haven't asked. I've asked, and I never get a clear answer. I think you would find many internal struggles in the schools over that issue."

Before he taught special education, Paul Osadchuk taught Grade 6. He told me it tore him up "to have to sit down over my lists and say, 'That kid has to go there, and that one there', and then to look at them in a couple of years and see what became of them." The sortout was one of his toughest and saddest jobs because he knew the blinders that snap on once a child is labeled "vocational". He told me, "Actually, I'm pretty lucky this year. Two are going AV. Last year I had to send five."

Placement is such a tricky thing, a teacher's status hinges partly on doing it well. Osadchuk and two fellow teachers made so many displacements at senior school their first year, they finally devised a failproof testing battery designed to place pupils properly, and it worked. "Two years ago when we sent our kids over, we did a fantastic job, we only goofed on one kid."

Parents must give their consent before a psychiatrist or psychologist can give individual tests to their child. From that point on, however, their awareness depends on their principal's openness and their own persistence. Parents are rarely welcome at Admission Board meetings; they are usually simply presented a solution. If there is any minority opinion on the Admission Board, this is never disclosed to the parent. Some individuals have taken matters in their own hands. Psychologist Furr, for example, won't write a report on a child without giving it to the parents. He is an exception.

Does it matter? Perhaps what the system decides for the child within the system is the best choice available, given the options. A parent can object to Vocational School placement, but the alternative is Grade 8 repeated over and over until age 16.

For all that, parents became wise to streaming as the Trefann Court complaint surfaced. They knew what consignment to vocational schools meant, and how richly undeserved it sometimes was. And yet, they knew too that the mechanics of streaming were only the outward structure of grading within the classroom. It was also the so-called Pygmalion effect, the inclination of pupils to fulfill the expectations of the teacher, combined with the clash of cultures between school and home, that tipped the scales for many children.

How does it work? Take the case of Roger Finlay, one of the five sons of Alfred and Marjorie Finlay.[10] Alfred works at a plumbing supply company on Parliament Street, and Marjorie keeps their home at the edge of Regent Park. Roger attends Brockton High School, much against his mother's will. He is her fourth son, an alert but anxious youngster who seemingly had every chance when he entered kindergarten at Sprucecourt Public School. But school somehow lost its grip, and by Grade 7 at Lord Dufferin Public School he was failed.

The kindergarten teacher found that Roger enjoyed music and singing, he "expressed his thoughts clearly" and he had "a very good general knowledge and a great deal to offer", but she added: "He often needs to be reminded to sit back and listen to the ideas of others."

His Grade 1 teacher gave him a D in music the first term, with the notation: "Is improving." By the end of Grade 1, his language deficiency seemed well established. The teacher gave him a B with the tepid comment: "Is doing his best." When Roger failed Grade 7, the teacher put it this way: "Roger has matured this year in his attitude and his work habits. To best utilize this he will be remaining at the same level where we wish him all the best."

This resigned little note, like a kindly epitaph on a pauper's grave, consigned Roger to his station in life. One cannot say that school was the only thing that thwarted Roger's native talents. One can only say that school helped lock Roger in. I talked to Roger's mother. "You can see it as

---

[10] The names are changed to prevent identification.

it goes on," she said wearily, looking over his report cards. "I know it now, I didn't then. I really feel that they held him down. My feeling is that if he had that much initiative in kindergarten, what happened? Somebody must have put a stop to it somewhere along the line."

Roger could not remember those early times at school. When I had asked if school didn't seem bright at first, his eyes glazed over and he couldn't say. Next day I was at City Hall, reporting on an eight-hour session of City Council for *The Globe and Mail*. A face popped over the bannister of the reporters' loft. It was Roger. He had skipped class at Brockton to see if I really was a news reporter.

McKeown answered the Trefann Court complaints about middle-class bias by admitting it. It was true, he said, that the schools' curriculum was not relevant to the inner-city child's own community. A child's "maximum potential" is developed at school, McKeown explained, "as it relates to his ability to succeed in the essentially middle-class world of higher education, business and industry."[11]

What this means is that, to learn to read and write, a child must accept the sensibilities of the bureaucracy that provides the schooling. In that process, a child's natural strengths are often lost. A child who rebels against this is going to stay in special education longer.

Often the system has tried to combat the hopeless natural feelings around this selection process to avoid having to change the process itself. As the Hall-Dennis Report put it so eloquently, it is tragic when a child comes to label himself a slow learner, retarded, or handicapped. "On the fringes of the happy crowd" — so the chapter on special education begins — "sits a lonely little boy confronted with the almost impossible task of finding his way through a bewildering world. He is frightened. He feels miserable. He is made to feel different."

[11] Report to the Toronto Board of Education, June 3, 1970, page 9.

If special education was to solve the problem of failure with a feeling of success, it wasn't taking very well with the Trefann Court Mothers. They called Opportunity Class "a harsh statement of inadequacy", and then delivered their own analysis of what happens:

> What we are increasingly led to think is that the school system — with Opportunity Class as its dead-end division — just isn't set up to be meaningful for our kids. It doesn't relate to the things they know about and care about. It doesn't touch the world as it's experienced by people who don't have much money, who are forced to take society's hard and boring jobs, who are constantly threatened by unemployment, who are harassed by welfare officials or the police. It doesn't understand what it means to be a person with integrity under these circumstances, or where you find life and friendship. So the kids slide away, and turn their minds and hearts off. And many of those who turn off the most end up in Opportunity Class.

But if special classes seem now to be a dead end, what went wrong, and why were they expanded so swiftly? Was it simply a mistake, or was it, in fact, a bureaucratic convenience, the most sensible way thought possible to deal with misfits in the system? To say this is not to dispute the motives of those who carried it out. "We really did believe they would be better off there," one psychologist told me. "They would be protected from the social abuse, and they would get more academic help. It makes sense logically because don't forget the pupil-teacher ratio was reduced by half. But it is one of those things that made sense logically but didn't work that way in life."

Chapter 5

ON HAVING TO READ

Thieves

As I sit and write my life on a piece of paper,
I turn my head to view what used to be mine.
The words, the rhythm, the pulse of life.
  I've been stabbed by my very own knife.
  For now I realize I should have concealed my dreams
  My life, the way I feel.
  For now my thoughts are peeled, stripped bare,
  Left to rot in the open air,
Left to reveal the beauty of life that once was mine,
My very own, belonging to me.
But now they have been stolen out of kindness to me
  I should never have let them see.

— Sue Buchanan, Grade 8
Queen Alexandra Public School, 1970.

The lowest reading group in a Grade 4 class at Dundas School is toiling through *Off to School*, a primer put out by Copp Clark Publishing Company Ltd. and approved by the Ministry of Education. It is exemplary in every respect. The illustrations go to such lengths of propriety as to have Father take off his hat in the Department Store.

If you take the pictures and stories as they are supposed to be taken, devoid of meaning, swept free of nuance, nothing could be cleaner. The first story is about Janet and John, who feed the pigs. John gets knocked over by a sow. "Look, John, look. Run, run. Run, John, run. Look, Janet, look. Come and help. Help! Help! Help!"

The pupils in this reading group, the lowest in the class, are called Rabbits. They are doing what another teacher at Dundas School told me never happens any more in Toronto schools. They are reciting the lesson. Their halting words come drifting over the third-floor classroom where the better reading groups, the Monkeys, Horses and Tigers, are engaged in other things. The lone teacher in this class of 28 hears the students recite with one ear, keeps a constant vigil with the other. It is the familiar litany of public schooling. The scene resounds with memories for anyone who learned to read at school.

The class moves on to Page 21, which says Janet needs help. The picture shows her about to drop an armful of packages. The teacher, trying to give them some conversational skills, asks the Rabbits why Janet needs help. Hands wave. Jimmy is permitted to reply. "She's got so many things she's going to drop some," the ten-year-old offers. He got it right. The Rabbits move on.

Another classroom in the same school gives another view of learning to read. Tom Marsh, a low-key, studious man, has one group of Grade 3 children doing whale projects.

"Linda's gone into dolphins," he comments, looking over her notebook. He asks why dolphins might be included.

"It has a hole in the top of its head," a child replies. "A dolphin breathes air, it's not really a fish."

"Here she has a shark," Marsh notes. "Do you think it still fits into a project on whales? I think so, as long as she points out that it's different."

On Having to Read

Linda has a pleased look on her face as he hands it back. He takes Jimmy's. "You don't look very happy with yours," Marsh tells him.

"I don't like the pictures, that's all," says Jimmy.

Marsh leafs through it. "Now one thing I like about Jimmy's is that he's used his own words. Remember what we said yesterday about copying right out of the book?"

Jimmy brightens.

As the lesson proceeds, a child walks up and asks to listen to another record at the listening station. It is permitted. Others are drawing pictures and words from the blackboard. Three paint, two run a filmstrip. Marsh meanwhile is taking questions about whales and writing them on the blackboard.

1. How to catch whales?
2. Why do we catch whales?
3. Whaling season.
4. Why does he live under the sea when he's a mammal?
5. Fresh water — salt water?

He asks where they'll be able to find all this, and writes down the sources: television, museum, books, thinking, people.

"People — who?" he asks.

"Somebody that catches whales," Jimmy replies.

Their assignment is to pick out one question and answer it for next time. Whales may be far removed from Dundas Street. It is "irrelevant," but I find myself getting interested in whales anyway. Marsh is a fine exponent of the project method, and his children are getting some of the worth of words in the process of practicing them. This teacher was drawing forth the language at their disposal, building on it, enriching it, showing them how to use it better.

Toronto schools are a disparate mixture of methods and

manners. In spite of all the methods, learning to read is still a mystery. It depends on all sorts of home variables, community variables, and personality traits, but part of it — a large part, it has been discovered — depends on the system in which it happens — or doesn't happen.

In 1968, the *Toronto Education Quarterly* published by the Board of Education printed this selection from the late social critic, Paul Goodman:

> A chief obstacle to children's learning to read is the present school setting in which they have to pick it up. For any learning to be skillful and lasting, it must be or become self-motivated, second-nature; for this, the schooling is too impersonal, standardized, and academic. If we tried to teach children to speak by academic methods in a school-like environment, many would fail and most would stammer.

Goodman, in his testimony to the Borough President of Manhattan in New York City, proposed "tiny schools, radically decentralized" as a solution to the grossly depersonalized educational structures in his own city. Within the tiny schools he proposed a natural, experiential reading method in which "reading and writing are gut-meaningful, they convey truth and feeling."

It was a good omen, to have published that in Toronto in 1968. This system was about to strike hard times over the failure of reading in the city schools.

During the late 1960's reading became a great anxiety. The fierce concern with mathematics and science had subsided with the 1950's. That had been a spill-over preoccupation anyway, from the post-Sputnik paranoia then at large in the United States. Canada, meanwhile, alarmed at a high level of unemployment and a 48 percent high school dropout rate, geared itself to a major expansion of vocational and technical schooling. The system expanded, the dropout rate fell. Children could stay in school longer, and they did.[1]

But staying in school was not learning to read. The high schools discovered that those who might have dropped out before were unable or unwilling to clear that first elementary hurdle. They couldn't read.

High school teachers complained loudly. One Toronto estimate, put together by the Basic Program Elements Sub-Committee in late 1973, said 50 percent of all secondary students needed special help in reading. The freeing up of the elementary curriculum, then in vogue in Ontario, often got the brunt of it. The elementary schools didn't seem to be doing the job any more. But in fact the trouble lay deeper.

The complaint had come not just from English department heads, but also from newly vocal inner-city parents. From Cabbagetown and Riverdale, those Anglo-Saxon lower working class and welfare communities, came the cry of parents who discovered the schools weren't giving them a fair break. Their great hope lay in education, but the lack of the merest ability to read kept them out. The middle-class schools had their failures, too, it was true. The steady beat of educational critics — Rudolf Flesch's *Why Johnny Can't Read*, in 1955, Hilda Neatby's *So Little for the Mind* in 1958, John Holt's *How Children Fail* in 1967 — kept the public alert and on edge. But whatever was happening in the middle-class communities that read those books, failure was epidemic in the inner city.

At Dundas Public School, for example, a full 60 percent of the Grade 5 pupils in 1972 were reading two years below the average, according to standardized tests. This was almost three times the "failure" rate in reading at the North

---

[1] By 1966, the dropout rate fell to one-fourth its 1959 level.

Toronto schools. This means, in crude statistical terms, that only one in three of the inner city pupils stood a chance of making it into an academic, technical or commercial secondary school. Two in three were destined to go vocational or "terminal." Admittedly Dundas was one of the lowest, but at Duke of York, a school that had been receiving compensatory aid for five years, three-fourths were reading below the average grade levels in Grades 1-6 during 1973-74.

Admittedly, too, the tests were faulty. To judge working class and welfare pupils by middle-class norms is patently deceptive and wrong. The system itself gamely admits this fact, but it goes on using them. And, ironically, the tests do correctly reflect the attitudes and values of the school system itself, and as such they had to be taken seriously as an index to success. If the ability to read formed the threshold to a public education, the standardized exam was its doorkeeper.

The system's attempts to come to terms with the problem of reading were tortured and slow. For starters, only a few trustees really wanted the facts to be known. The early attempts of Trustee Graham Scott of inner-city Ward 7 to get the officials to publish the reading scores at all schools met solid resistance. Their desire for specific, accurate information simply wasn't strong enough to take the risk of showing up some schools in very bad light. The administrators talked the trustees out of this notion. It seemed bad enough to compare pupils against each other at school, but to measure school against school was unthinkable; the sensibilities of those in charge were at stake.

The Fundamental Skills Committee at the behest of the administrators, forbade "any form of testing which would be used for comparison between schools" in the spring of 1970. The board confirmed this action and instructed the

Research Department to do a major study on reading proficiency and socio-economic status. By the time the study was done Scott had decided to quit the board. He commented: "The board simply wouldn't come to grips with the problem of basic skills."

Yet a few things did come to light in September 1972, when the Research Department's study became public. Donald Rutledge, head of the Language Study Centre at the time, called it "the good news report," and Edgar Wright, director of research, summed it up in these words: "There's no room for complacency in this data. I think, though, that people who say Toronto is a disaster area are incorrect." The study generally showed that Toronto students read about as well as average American pupils do on the Gates-MacGinitie Reading Test. They rated no better and no worse, once the new immigrant children had been excluded from the returns.

This may have been solace to harried administrators; it was hardly any comfort to those living in the less fortunate parts of town. Their plight became brutally clear when Wright used his socio-economic data from the Every Student Survey of 1970 to compare the well-to-do families with the poor. A typical taxi driver's youngster in Grade 8 was about a year behind average. All along the line, children's reading abilities fell as their socio-economic level declined.

The principal judge in this case, the Gates-MacGinitie Reading Test, was an instrument put together in the United States. It was rigorously standardized, designed to sort out pupils by the sweep of their vocabularies and their powers of comprehension, couched securely in the middle class milieu of schooling. The results were predictable, telling the likes of the Trefann Court Mothers that Toronto was little worse than anywhere else. The poor had done no worse than expected.

But the researchers pushed their study one step further.

They attempted to get beyond the standardized response by sampling the pupils' ability to write original prose. They had the teachers select two average essays from 526 pupils in Grade 8. Then they had three highly skilled high school teachers rate them by clarity of ideas, grammar, originality and organization. The papers were not identified by school or author, so that the inner city essays could rise or fall on their own merits — given, of course, the cultural bias of the three high school teachers. The study revealed that the lower-class pupils rated only slightly lower than their upper-class peers. Their "handicaps" didn't interfere as much with their ability to get across a message as it did with their ability to rate high on the tests.

In the late winter of 1970, the Park School Council pressured the principal to make public the reading scores, and the result was another rear-guard skirmish on the reading crusade. He complied in February 1971; the results were shocking. The scores showed that 42 percent of the Grade 8 pupils were two years or more below grade level, even exempting the children already consigned to slow learner classes.

"We feel the figures are damning enough to speak for themselves," the Trefann Court Mothers said in a letter to the board. "We demand that the Toronto Board of Education give special attention to the Grade 8 pupils of Park School and that a crash program to upgrade their reading level be implemented immediately."

Hastily, the board jerked into action. On April 29, ten days after getting that letter, the Board of Education decided "that an intensified program in remedial reading and language development be instituted at Park Public School-Senior forthwith." So it was that all the Grade 8 pupils had to take yet another Gates-MacGinitie Reading Test in late April, and all but the best found themselves consigned to an intensified program to end all intensified programs. Eight special language consultants descended on the school. They got $700 worth of books, and all the equipment they wanted. The consultants immediately found that the students' attitude towards reading was "extremely negative." To overcome the resistance they provided some of the most fetching stuff available such as *Tryst, Sam & Me, Skinny, Puzzle in Purple, This Thing Called Love,* and *Fullback Fury.* For poetry they tried *Reflections on a Gift of Watermelon Pickle, On City Streets,* and several Simon and Garfunkle selections.

The consultants said they were greeted with, "You're the one who's come to teach us stupid kids how to read" and "this is nothing but dumb charity" and "I'll come and I'll do what you say but I won't read". It was not a propitious start, but after seven weeks, one consultant reported "a marked change in attitude toward reading and myself." Some had read books all the way through for the first time, and they showed some interest. But not for long.

The board had asked its Research Department to measure the success of this crash program. So the researchers tested them against a control group of 98 other poor readers. It turned out that the reading comprehension of the controls fell back three months during those closing weeks of Grade 8, while the Park School pupils merely held their own, and gained a little in vocabulary.

But the biggest loss was the examination itself. "The roof collapsed when they arrived June 22 to be tested," the consultant wrote. "They showed a complete turnabout in their approach to the class. The tests were, in all cases, left incomplete and they didn't care about the results or how the results would affect them."

The researchers concluded in their final report that most of the children felt judged and condemned as stupid. "An intensive program of less than two months cannot produce significant changes in language and reading skills, which are cumulative from birth," they said. "What is needed at Park School, as at all schools, is ongoing, quiet, concentrated attention to the language and reading program at all levels." Which is what these 42 children had been getting during their previous eight years at school.

One conclusion drawn from the failure of the inner city child to measure up in the school system is the insufficiency of his speech patterns. This is usually laid to the culture of poverty, rather than to intelligence, though it is a common myth in the Toronto system that inner city children don't naturally have it. Their failure at reading no doubt does stem from the strains of poverty, the insecurity of broken homes, the misery of malnourishment and disordered living conditions. For none of these things are the children at fault, and their families too are victims of society's neglect and willful ignorance. But when it comes to speaking, the theory that the poor don't get as much practice ought to be looked at very critically.

This point of view is sometimes traced to the work of social psychologist Basil Bernstein. He pointed out the mismatch of the language used at school and the language used at home. He found that working-class kids use concrete, simple language, while middle-class kids are more inclined to abstract, complex, speech. That much is accepted, but more recent theorists made the Bernstein theory into cultural imperialism by saying the poor need to be brought up to standard. The implication was that their direct, simple talk results from lack of challenge and scope, that therefore they are cut off from a world of learning that is open to the middle-class child. It is not that simple. As much of a case could be made for the argument that their simple, direct speech gets them places the school system doesn't want them to go, therefore it systematically robs them of it.

True, the lower working-class and the middle-class talk different languages. But Toronto provides a few shreds of evidence that the inner-city poor use words at least as well as their well-to-do counterparts. A study at Sackville Public School, located at the southern edge of Cabbagetown, assessed the "talkability" of 15 pre-schoolers who had come to take part in a new Montessori program. In this case, the researchers didn't administer any tests. They simply sat and listened for an hour and recorded what they heard. They did the same at an uptown nursery of upper middle-class kids.

The results gave a surprising new insight into the contrasts between upper and lower economic groupings. For one thing, the inner-city children talked more than the uptowners did. Their vocabularies were the same size, but the inner-city children produced half again as many words in one hour. And the Sackville children were far more demanding. This is how Carol Reich, the researcher, described it:

> Upon entering the Sackville classroom, a visitor would soon be surrounded and pulled in all directions by different children wanting him to watch what they were doing. It was very difficult to work with any one child because other children would constantly be trying to engage the visitor in conversation. When this researcher asked individual children to accompany her outside the classroom in order to be tested, most were eager to comply. And the testing itself was frequently accompanied by chatter and conversation.
>
> The same visitor could very likely spend the entire morning with the uptown group without being approached by a single child. When asked to accompany the researcher for the testing, although agreement was eventually elicited, it was less than enthusiastic and often obtained only after repeated requests.

The tests were simple pairing exercises, and all the children became thoroughly bored with them. The researchers had to resort to candy rewards to keep them at it. In the end, the uptown children rated higher, though they all did about the same on the first run through. The downtown kids got worse as the test went on, while the uptowners gradually improved. It seems the uptowners knew how to knuckle in and make it in the system, which hardly answers the question of who really was smarter. Carol Reich reported:

> The uptown children continued to work at the disagreeable task. They sat quietly in their chairs and concentrated. The Sackville children on the other hand were restless. Their attention constantly wandered to other objects in the room. Many of them tried to engage the tester in conversation. This was one situation in which the downtown children were very verbal in contrast to the uptown group, but their use of language actually interfered with intellectual performance.

Too bad, but the test doesn't seem to have been something a sensible child would sit still for. The eagerness of these children to talk, if the system were ready for it, seems to indicate a fine opportunity to let them learn.[2]

One thing the consultants learned out of all this was that many inner city children who aren't reading simply refuse to read. If the system won't accept their language, the least they can do is reject the school's language, and that seems to be the key to a lot of reading problems. This became clear as Donald Rutledge talked about the Park School crash program:

---

[2] "Preschool Education for Inner-City Children: Preliminary Results of an Experimental Montessori Programme," by Carol Reich, Research Department, Toronto Board of Education, November 1971.

There were very few of those youngsters, even those who scored Grade 3 and Grade 4 level in reading, who couldn't read. They didn't *want* to read. I say that in my report to the board.

They don't want to read, in fact, they almost *dare* you to teach them to read. And if you build a relationship with them its something like that poem (*Thieves*, by Sue Buchanan) where you're almost seducing them away from the life that they know.

And I began to think about this, and so did all of us who were involved, and I realized that if I were in their position, perhaps at an unconscious level I might do the same. Because unconsciously, they know that if they go into this book learning stuff, into all that 'high falutin' stuff, they are going to get into professions that encourage shallow breathing.

And they're going to get away from the world they grew up in, to put it very simply. I don't know if you were at the Park meeting where we almost had a riot, the big one? There was a youngster who spoke there and it was heartrending, and he said he made it through Park, and he made it through Jarvis, and he was at University.

And he said 'I don't know what it is but they're different from me. And actually I don't get on too well at home either because they think I'm talking, you know 'uppity' at home.' And in *The Excitement of Writing* over there, which comes out of Yorkshire riding in England, they have a piece of writing by a kid who said exactly the same thing. He comes from a working class background and makes it to Oxford, he can't enter a room the way the kids from Rugby can. And they know it and he knows it. And he goes home and they hate him because he talks 'posh'.

The irony is that a lot want to keep that vitality, well they wouldn't put it that way, but they also want the impersonal language of expository prose and I come back to my question, 'Is it necessary to lose one to gain the other?' I don't think so. But I don't think we have worked out a method that accommodates itself to the raw gutsiness of that kind of talk and at the same time allows people to develop.

Then we got into the kinds of texts most schools use. Rutledge said he found it good to use authors like William Blake and Christina Rossetti, or to get into the Norse myths. He saw no need to stuff inner-city children with Dr Suess, much less Jack and Jill.

I had gone to the library in the Mowat Block at Queen's Park, where the Ministry of Education keeps a rack of all the books approved as texts for Ontario school, and reviewed the readers. Here is a sampling of what I found.

There was *Off to School*, the book published by Dent that the Dundas School reading group had been reciting. I was tantalized by the fact that pupils who graduate from *Off to School* can go on to another Dent publication, *Developing Comprehension in Reading*, which begins with this introduction:

> All boys and girls *want* to be good readers.
> All girls and boys *need* to be good readers. Do you know why?
> Stop and think. How many times do you use reading in one day? It is a good many times. There are so many ways to use reading. . . .
> This book has many stories. Some are funny. Some tell about something new. All of them were written to help you be a better reader.

Having done with Dent, I went on to a Ginn Integrated Language Program that has probably become the most popular series in Toronto primary grades. It is built around the sanguine adventures of Mugs, an oversized dog. Determinedly exciting, current and middle-class, *What A Dog* gives this sequence as an updated version of Dick-and-Jane:

>Look, Mommy.
>A jet!
>Mommy look!
>Here comes a jet!
>Here it comes Mommy!

Another favorite of Toronto schools is the Nelson Language Development Reading Program, beginning with *Funny Surprises*. This book edges gradually toward reading with 15 pages of pictures and nursery rhymes. A child will hear, respond, and then start to read. The stories build into work activities. A story of a fish develops into drawing animals, labeling them and displaying them on the bulletin board.

And then there was *Listening Letters*, part of the Language Patterns Series of Holt, Rinehart and Winston of Canada, Ltd. This is a "sounding out" reader, and not a bad one. For once, it overcomes the pedantic "look look" tone of so many readers.

The first word is "Sam," under a picture of a dog. "Sit Sam!" is next, and then "Sam sits." These are words a child might identify with. Next, under a stylized picture of a boy: "This is Tim. Tim sits." And then still another dog, this one very droopy eyed. "This is Matt. Matt is Tim's." I found it totally unpatronizing. It was a reading text without corn syrup. Several teachers at the Ottawa Public School Board wrote it.

There were many more, some better, some worse. In the classrooms I found the teachers had enriched the fare with imports of all varieties. But the best readers are the ones the children themselves wrote. At Huron Street Public School, the staff binds the books as children write and illustrate them.

However they do it, the necessary thing is that the words make sense of a child's situation. Educators often describe the situation of poverty as one that must be alleviated in order for children to learn, when what is needed is to learn how to change the situation by the use of language. A developmental approach could foster this, but unfortunately the schools are not very inclined to do it. Their own structures are too authoritarian to allow that sort of power to be the core of a reading program.

The Park School Council caught onto this by reference to the work of Paulo Friere, the Latin American educator who wrote *The Pedagogy of the Oppressed*. They published this selection from *The Paulo Friere Method* in a report from the council's reading subcommittee in June 1971:

> While the Paulo Friere method assumes that themes of national importance play a role in the development of a critical mentality, it also assumes that the presentation of them should be linked to the personal, local problems of the person seeking education. . . Conscientizacao means an "awakening of consciousness", a change of mentality involving an accurate, realistic awareness of one's locus in nature and society; the capacity to analyse critically its causes and consequences, comparing it with other situations and possibilities; and action of a logical sort aimed at transformation.

It was hardly the kind of thing to be found in the official or unofficial readers, but at Jesse Ketchum School I found one teacher introducing something like that.

She was Grace Lee and she taught Grade 1. She had her class make up a big chart telling where the children eat lunch. They did it on a graph, getting their first lesson in statistics. "The children who ate at school — they were the fewest — kept hopping up twice to be counted, so somebody suggested we just count the lunch boxes," Mrs Lee said. Seventeen ate lunch at a day care centre, nine ate at school, four ate at home. The class had done a social analysis of itself, incomplete and innocent, but it made sense because it told about themselves. Mrs Lee does other things like that, more from an intuitive sense of interest than from any theories about learning. She has her class describe their mothers' work, carefully types their comments on large sheets of paper, then has them draw illustrations. She posts them all in the hallway under the blazing banner: "My Mommy Works Hard Too." No grades attached, no judgments made.

Parents in the inner city by and large have had enough of experimentation. They want their children to learn to read and write. They have little stomach for programs of personality enrichment, exploration and discovery, which strike them as middle class games they haven't time for. In the pressurized setting of inner city schools, with frightened suburban teachers in charge, the language experience approach can prove the parents right: it can evolve into chaos. "The result can be classroom anarchy, and I abhor that as much as I do 30 students in six rows," one teacher told me. "I wouldn't even call it just an inferior program, I would say it's damaging to children."

But if it is done well, the language experience program lets children speak their own idiom, building on the gifts they bring with them to school. The trouble is that it can hardly be done well in Toronto, the way the schools are set up.

The schools' insistence on propriety of language emasculates not merely the inner city child; it is only blatantly evident there. Any child who fears to express his feelings in the school, or who knows that certain words and ideas are taboo, is caught in the web of conformity and powerlessness.

I once thought writing lines as punishment had gone the way of the hickory stick, but I was wrong about that. In one Grade 3 class, William carefully printed William Works Well ten times on a sheet of wide-ruled paper. This teacher made no apology; it was his way, and I took him to be a fine teacher. In another school, a special education teacher had his children — all of them boys, as is often the case in behavioral classes — "do their lines" as one of the milder forms of punishment. He, too, was a good teacher, much too enlightened to think writing lines had any hortatory benefit in itself. "That's a lot of crap," he told me. "If a boy writes those lines, all it means is he accepts my authority."

Language study. Almost anything that goes on in the classroom can be language study, especially in a freed-up classroom. Teachers take their on-the-moment chances. John, a Grade 1 pupil at Ossington in Toronto's west end, had spent the morning making himself a cardboard sword and shield. He described it proudly, pronouncing "shield" as "sield". Without a hitch, the teacher, Marjorie Fonck, wrote the word on the blackboard, pointed out the "sh," pronounced it correctly. "Yeah," John said, "and I'm going to make a helmet tomorrow." She had put across a whole lesson in pronunciation, spelling and phonics in 15 seconds.

But it takes alert, mature teachers. The freed-up classroom offers so much chance for acting out — on the part of both teachers and students — that many deteriorate into aimlessness or hysteria.

Rutledge noted that many teachers claim not to need a structure. "They do need a structure," he attests, "but not a structure that is arbitrarily reached. They need a structure that grows out of what's happening, that reflects the needs of the entire group. I've visited classes where the teacher was trying to be developmental, but the children were just kept at a high pitch, at the edge of hysteria, all day long. And they called it developmental. You can really knock the whole thing on this point of aimlessness. To teach in an open fashion requires a very good teacher, but I think to advise anything else is a counsel of despair."

Once all the newest and best theories are expounded, you are left with basic truths. Principal James Donnelly and I sat in his little study at Old Orchard School one November morning talking about reading. We had gone over the theories. Donnelly, a short, intense man who exudes an inner calm, began where I requested with a review of good and bad reading books. "As a general rule," he told me, "a good book is a book the child is really interested in. It ought to be well illustrated, and it ought to deal with the range of experience a child knows."

This was elemental; we were dealing in truisms. "I think that nobody really understands the reading process. For all the studying that's been done, it's still largely a mystery. It's still true that no one method stands out. If you'd ask me how a child can learn to read, I'd still say, Get a good teacher. That's the primary thing. What works with some children doesn't work with others, so you have to keep open.

"But I do have preferences.

"At Ossington School we had what you might call a language experience approach. A better term for it might be the developmental program. We recognize that learning to read is a highly personal thing . . . "

Donnelly went on to expound the views of Frank Smith, a professor at the Ontario Institute for Studies in Education, who describes reading as an exchange. The reader brings to the page his own experience, and the more he brings, the more he gets back from the page. But if the language is one the child has not experienced, he must depend entirely on the page itself. He cannot really read it; he must decode it.

Donnelly called on the experts again. Dorothy Heathcote in England, who found through drama that children could claim their emotional heritage and express true feelings. Northrop Frye, who in *The Educated Imagination* said we need to begin at the core of any discipline and work outward, the core of language being poetry. "We miss a great deal if we don't read poetry every day," said Donnelly.

An hour had gone. He began to sense that I understood all that. Arrogant-newsman-meets-innovative-administrator gave way to two persons inquiring into learning. The defenses mellowed. "Writing will come, I'm sure of that," he said. "What's most important for the child is to be able to give back a response, and for it to be accepted. You know, I started out in this business as a phys ed teacher, and that's when I first realized that some children sometimes have to articulate their experience and feelings in body movement before they can do it in speech and writing. We had some people from England telling us children's dance and play counts for something. At first we sat back and scoffed, but then we began to look at what was happening to the kids, and sure enough, they were articulating things they never would have had the words for, and after that they found the words."

A perilous, unpredictable endeavor, learning to read and write. It is too delicate to be entrusted blindly to just any new technique. We talked about open education, its values and dangers. "In order to learn at age 6 or 8, a child generally needs an environment that is less ambiguous, less threatening," Donnelly said. "He already has to contend with 30 peers and one dominating adult. But put him in an open area and he has at least 60 peers and two or three dominating adults.

"This increases the difficulties. The child can learn to use language as a defensive tool. He can learn to use words to *shut out* the environment. What we are trying to do is help him use words to *explore* the environment. The child needs to be able to expose himself to the teacher, he needs to reveal himself, and to do that he needs to feel very secure."

A teacher pushed the door open to remind Donnelly of a staff meeting at 12:15. I knew we had just begun, but that seemed to be the nub of it right there.

Chapter 6

DOING IT IN HIGH SCHOOL

Is virginity obsolete?
   Not yet.
What is meant by the double standard?
   I haven't the faintest idea.
Why isn't there a pill for men?
   Yeah, why isn't there?
What gave you MOST of the information you presently have on the topic of sex education?
   Myself.
Is the pill difficult to obtain?
   Not difficult enough.
What is an I.U.D.?
   Interviral Urinal Devise.
How does the diaphragm, as a method of birth control, function?
   Helps push baby out.
What is the population of Port Credit?
   Increasing.
Why don't human beings produce litters?
   Because they aren't four-legged creatures.
Deformed babies should not be allowed to live.
   True.
How effective is the condom?

Not so effective because it could up and leak.
Use the remaining paper to list some of the areas you feel should be discussed.
All of them.

— Questions and answers culled from a questionnaire given to a Grade 11 class at the start of a unit on Birth Control and Family Planning at Humberside Collegiate Institute.

The topic is birth control.

Twenty-three students in Grade 11 file merrily into Pat Kincaid's classroom on the third floor of Humberside Collegiate Institute. Some bring essays that are due today on contraception, abortion, euthanasia, sperm banks, pornography, sterilization, family planning, eugenics, sex education, artificial insemination, or simply, "Your choice of topic — related to this course".

Jim has written "Pornography, What is It?" He puts his paper on the desk and takes a chair near the front.

Pat Kincaid, health and physical education teacher, divides her class into discussion groups. Each student receives a ditto sheet with five problems. The first: "In spite of the availability of contraceptives, the abortion rate remains high. What are some of the reasons for this?"

The students push their chairs into five little groups; Jim finds himself with Jeanette and Mary. After an uneasy cough and some light banter, Jeanette risks saying that abortion goes unabated because people think it spoils an affair to use contraceptives. Jim does a comedy routine on how hard it is to get a box of condoms at the local druggist when the sales clerk is a girl you happen to know. "It's just embarrassing, that's all."

By common consent, they pass over the next question. "It's too hard," Jim says. They all nod. The question: "Parents who become upset and angry when their children masturbate are mishandling the situation." This touches closer than abortion or contraceptives. The next question asks whether deformed babies should be killed. It is a fine challenge; the two girls get into an argument.

Mary is for mercy killing. "If you let them live they just put them in institutions," she says, "and in institutions they keep kids in cages. No institution has the time to baby a kid."

Jeanette: I don't think they should be put in institutions, not unless they're hopeless.

Mary: Well, these *are*. Like I mean if you already have two kids, and there's a mentally retarded kid born in the family, you have enough already. You can't take it.

Jim shifts uneasily. His books spill out on the floor. They are *Perspectives on Pornography, Lord of the Flies, Mathematics II,* and a fat looseleaf book of notes. He stuffs them back.

Jeanette: You're still responsible for it. You can't give it up.

Mary: Not if you put it in an institution, you're not responsible. An institution takes all responsibility.

Jeanette, angrily: You're treating them like animals.

Mary: Our society treats them like animals. Our society isn't prepared to hold them, so why should you?

Jeanette: You mean you do what society tells you to do?

Mary: No. Everybody does. Society will look down on you. I know you will have feelings about it but . . .

The argument rages through half the period until finally they leave it for the fourth question, whether sex education encourages young people to be sexually active before they're ready. The consensus is that it doesn't.

"In Grade 5," Jim says, "you laugh about it. Big words, you know. I remember on the way home from school, intercourse was the new word everybody was talking about. We didn't know what it was, but everybody was using the new word. And later on, the girls heard about having the period, and then the new word was menstruation."

Whereupon the period was up. The students pushed their chairs into rows. Jim went off to mathematics. "They're different, all right, maths and birth control. They're different."

It had been 40 minutes of open talk in a nine-period academic day. They had expressed themselves and heard others talk, been stirred and ruffled, been made to think out loud for a moment about sex. It had been a brief stay.

"This is the point at which I'd like to have them another three weeks," Pat Kincaid told me. "We spend two weeks just getting into it, and giving them some background, and then it's over. Tomorrow is the last day."

Sex education in many Toronto schools is an isolated attempt to bring life and school together. The first sentence in the school system's climate-setting guide for sex education describes the problem: "In a school culture where personal competition is keen, suspicion of others high, and evaluation by a teacher inevitable, a student will be hesitant to talk about himself." This guideline, *Human Relations in Health Education*, came out of Suite 555, at the west end of a gray matte hallway, a gaily disordered corner inside the otherwise spick-and-span Education Centre.

I sat there at a cluttered table, Robert Gladish, director of health and physical education, directly opposite, and Gloria Torrance, a health consultant, at my left. Can any good thing come out of Nazareth, I'm thinking. The phys ed department, territory of jocks, those non-academic whiz kids who work their way into vice-principalships, those football coaches who hold the reputations of schools in their hands. My presuppositions were wrong; out of the locker room there shone a great light. Learning is a tender personal affair, even at high school. Sensitivity has to be shown it. The structures have to bend and break, the old formalities must yield. During the late 1960's, the sex educators of Toronto discovered that what was wrong with most sex education was just what was wrong with most sex — the absence of communication.

"The first day of health felt to me like the first day of school," a Grade 12 boy said in retrospect, thinking back on a communications sequence in the health program at Jarvis Collegiate Institute. It was the start of an unsettling two weeks of role playing, simulated Moon journeys, sign language games, making lists of "15 things I love doing," and writing a retrospective diary at the end. This was part of the new sensitivity, and it worked. One girl wrote: "I'm sure a lot of people don't realize what they're doing and just live each day a bore."

It was teacher Craigie McQueen's class. She walked in, closed the door, sat down and said nothing for five minutes. It was to jar students loose from their routine expectations, make them wonder and think. Afterward they wrote down their feelings. "It shows how we really can't get together without the teacher starting us off," one girl wrote, "the reason being because we have had so many years of class training, and the students were all wondering what was going on because it was an unusual way to start a class."

It was not strictly sex education. But classes like these took in the wide world of human emotion to give sex education a place at school. "How can you talk about sexuality if you're all a bundle of nerves, you're all strung out, and you don't know each other at all?" That was Robert Gladish, who took over the health and physical education department in 1971, just as the new curriculum burst on the system. The department had a corner on sex education, but as it burgeoned the subject seemed crudely out of place in the ordinary school format. The way had to be prepared for it. "I think that problems of sexuality can only be looked at if the climate has been set properly," said Gloria Torrance.

And at Humberside Collegiate Institute, there was John

Michaluk teaching about sexuality in a former cafeteria, four tattered rugs on the floor, a blackboard at one wall, a few desk-chairs scattered around, students all seated on the floor. He had set the climate. Other schools seemed to push sex education to one side; perhaps that was just as well. They monopolized on the unorthodox space. At Central Technical School they used the tool room of the carpentry shop; at Castle Frank High School they use a windowless furnace room. Most schools, though, just used ordinary classrooms; the liberties of Humberside and Jarvis caught on slowly. But freedom of that sort upsets the stereotype a great grey school system will endure gladly. The sensitivity bash came and went in the late 1960's, leaving many health teachers with the "touchy-feely" image to live down. But in sex education they were not interested in simply getting off on gimmicks; this was serious necessity, the environment had to change, the curriculum had to unwind. The subject demanded something else.

Sex education came to life in Toronto about 1966. Out of the sterile official womb came a delicate cuckoo, and nobody quite knew what it would grow up to be. The head of phys ed at the time was Charles Prince, a man ill at ease with the new creature; he broached that first sex curriculum gingerly, hoping to avoid an inevitable flood of parental outrage. "We knew it was a hot potato and we didn't want to make a big issue out of it," he said at the time. He need not have worried. Except for the steady harangues of Mahlon Beach, a school trustee down on sex education, the public seemed unperturbed. When south of the border the sex education controversy rated a 10-part series in the *Christian Science Monitor,* the Toronto Board of Education did its thing quietly. The key was caution. "That's the way Toronto does things," Gladish remarked. "For every five things we do, we get at least four of them right." Sex education seemed to be one of the four. Its success lay largely in the constancy of Gloria Torrance, and the aggressiveness of Peter Robertson, two consultants who burned away nights and days to give Toronto the finest set of family life kits and sex education guidelines on the Canadian market.

The 1966 beginning entailed the introduction of a family life curriculum in Grades 7-12, and the hiring of four consultants. "Family Life" sounded sufficiently domestic, allowing school trustees to approve it without great ado. "I hope we can divest it of the title of sex education," Board chairman Barry Lowes was heard to say. "That has an unwholesome ring to it. The course will be much more than that." He was right about it being much more than that, but the consultants the trustees hired had other notions about unwholesome rings. When the 1972 sex guideline was ready, it carried the proud title, *Human Sexuality*. And when the Family Life Kit was assembled, it included seven contraceptive devices and a plastic pelvis.

Until this time, the official mention of sex at school was often wrapped in academic obscurities, or blithely ignored. Thus does *Maturing in a Changing World*, the Ministry's approved text, tell about sexual behavior and arousal: "Sexual *arousal* is influenced by hormones, sensory stimulation, and by the higher centres in the brain. For the execution of sexual behavior, the role of hormones is negligible; external stimuli and brain mechanisms are of prime importance." All a kid needs to know. Another text for Grade 12 or 13, entitled *Families*, leaves a curious vacuum in describing the joys of parenthood: "The responsibility — and the fun — of bringing up children begins the day the doctor confirms the good news." And not a moment before. In addition to these evasions, the sex program had a strong moral undertone, as exemplified by Prince's first curriculum guide of 1968. "Is some sex play normal?" teachers were advised to ask students. "Is there a point of no return?

Whose responsibility is it to set limits?" This edged suggestively close to the rather tedious games adults play with sex, dealing more with titillation than sexuality.

The new guideline jumped into the thick of sexual matters with little sidestepping or playing prude. It did not quite attain the utter candor of *The Little Red Schoolbook*, a Danish import, but it certainly stopped nowhere short of giving all the necessary facts.[1] A youngster is advised where condoms should be bought, a helpful side benefit of learning it in school: "Select a drug store where the turnover would be adequate and the quality good." The guide observes that the Pill makes possible premarital sex without fear of pregnancy. It says the removal of fear will deepen sexual life, but adds that sexual freedom "can also be a question of deciding not to do something." It reviews the churches' views on birth control, and introduces hard questions, such as "What are some genuine reasons for having children?" and "Should birth control ever be compulsory?" The new guide is immersed in factual data and moral issues, full of life and spontaneous thoughts, covering a broad range of auxilliary books and films, including Mary Von Stolk's *The Battered Child in Canada* and the film *Sexuality and Communication* by Ontario's famous sex educators, Beryl and Avinoam Chernick.[2] All of this, of

---

[1] From *The Little Red Schoolbook*'s section on masturbation, this delightfully disarming selection on the four-letter words: "The usual word for a boy's sexual organ is cock or prick. The usual word for a girl's sexual organ is pussy or cunt. Many grown-ups don't like these words because they say they are 'rude'. They prefer words like penis and vagina."

[2] This film is built on lectures and role-playing, but is very explicit, as when a married woman asks if she should masturbate and is told, "Most women do it, and when you're frustrated, like you are, I think it's a very natural way to relieve the frustration." The film has been shown without objection at most schools, though at one, Jarvis Collegiate, the staff decided it wasn't appropriate for the course.

course, was only in the teacher's guide, not directly accessible to students. But it gave teachers full discretion. The Family Life Kit, a small suitcase of pamphlets, film strips and information posters, also contained samples of all the birth control devices. Nothing took the mystique out of the condom or the diaphragm like passing them around the class and having a discussion about their proper use.

One thing that bothered Lowes and the other trustees at the start was their taking over such a vital function of the home. Lowes felt the home was "the best place to teach a child about sex", but as a matter of fact, the homes had failed. Girls were getting pregnant partly because they didn't know to insist on the condom, or how to use the Pill. Teaching it at school would at least combat the anarchy of the back seat, and teachers seemed stuck with it, as phys ed teacher Judy Skelton put it, "because we teachers are just the most available group of adults the kids have." And so the school rushed in where the home and the church feared to tread, leaving some troublesome questions unanswered.

Sex education had its critics from the very start. On one side was Trustee Mahlon Beach, a small, wizened publisher of Masonic literature, first elected in 1960 in the Beaches, who built his 12-year tenure out of an undying fight against sex education and creeping communism. Nothing drew him on like a hint of laxity, though it must be mentioned that his speeches included a tiny grin at the jeering gallery, as if to say, "I've got to do this, you've got to do that." He made himself a brittle foil for sex education by linking it with godless communism, yet his homespun bias held an iota of truth, as when he quoted Norman Vincent Peale as saying "sex is the most powerful and explosive force within us", and when he pleaded, "it is not the responsibility of the state to teach sex . . . marriage is a private and sacred matter . . . talking about sex in school cheapens it . . ."[3] He at least took the whole thing seriously.

[3] *The Toronto Telegram,* November 17, 1966, story by Leslie Gray.

It was Beach's brand of objection that Pat Kincaid had in mind when she assigned as an essay topic for her Grade 11 class this statement: "Sex education in schools only encourages young people to experiment sexually, because the approach is so clinical. Morality is swept aside in a sea of facts and figures."

A larger concern had to do with the avowed sanitizing of sex. Another critic, Trustee Ernest Barr, humanist pamphleteer and lay analyst, raised an attack from the antipsychiatric left. His jarring, declamatory methods made him into Beach's opposite number at the board. But what he wrote struck a deep attack at sex education for being abstractified, mechanistic and alien. "Better no sex education than alienated and irrelevant sex education, which costs the taxpayer money but does nothing to enlighten the child," he wrote in a letter to *The Globe and Mail*. "If sex education merely means teaching the child that chickens come from eggs and babies from mummy's tummy, and that abortions are illegal in Canada but drug companies have produced some dandy devices for birth control, then let us leave this subject to the street corner academy, which has done such a marvelous job of miseducating our children in this field in the past."

In fact, many sex educators did see themselves called upon to demythologize sex of its street-corner bogies by making it cleanly clinical. One advisor saw the need to rescue children from "the steamy scene of hilarious, risque dirty jokes" and an instructor's manual used at Jarvis Collegiate declared that even a poor sex education program was better than leaving it to "the locker room, pornographic magazines, and motion pictures and the commercial world that constantly exploits human sexuality."[4] Their concern was valid, and they did not intend to make sex sterile by laying it on at school. But what was the effect?

---

[4] *Instructor's Manual for Education for Sexuality* by John Burt and Linda Brower, W.B. Saunders Co., 1970, page 7.

Two girls at Jarvis Collegiate complained to Joan Skrlac, health teacher, that at school it didn't seem natural. "This is the type of thing we talk about outside the school," she recalled them saying, "Who do you think you are, asking us to talk about it in school, in this setting?"

The school could yet prove to stifle sexuality more thoroughly than home and church ever did. Simply by desensitizing relationships, by alienating boy or girl from true feeling, by resorting to *Playboy* permissiveness or to academic head games, sexuality could be undercut. The gleaming enamel reassurances of the Masters and Samuel sex labs, or the comfort of the Kinsey-Ellis general norms — these are weak substitutes for self knowledge.

The new sex curricula recognize this; it is doubtful that the schools do. Their reliance on a mechanistic view of human reality was illustrated by one phys ed teacher who hoped to install a bio-feedback machine next year to teach students about body responses — "hitch the kids up and see if they can, in fact, relate what they're feeling." She told me drugs were taboo but the bio-feedback machine, with its wires, meters and dials, seemed a viable, exciting alternative. Sex educators contend with a larger impersonal order; they don't entirely succeed. Teacher-student relations must fit into a system that is still heavily authoritarian. One teacher who conducted a sensitivity seminar did the class the final indignity of grading their diaries. To get an A plus, as one student did, entailed an enormous outpouring of personal feeling. It seemed an extraordinary way to earn an A.

Another problem is the 40-minute time slot during which sex education was to be taught. Every sex educator I asked told me the 40-minute period was an arbitrary, harmful arrangement. "Absolutely horrendous," said Joan Skrlac at Jarvis. "You just get into the height of the content and then you have to cut it." I asked if her department had tried to change it. "It's impossible. In the structure of the school, in a three-week unit, it just can't be done. It would upset the whole timetable of the school."

The 40-minute period seems to be an inevitable handicap to sustained relationships, be they over English literature, computer science or population control. The schools impose a certain promiscuity of human contact. Students seem languidly adapted to it, moving in and out of human groupings to the sound of bells. But they seemed hardly serious about learning; it was a treadmill to be walked, joyfully if possible.

But in espousing the need for climate setting, the health and physical education people did at least recognize sex as more than mechanics. Aside from techniques, which are soon learned, students wanted to explore the emotions. "They don't care so much about ovaries and fallopian tubes and the menstrual cycle. I think they're more concerned about their feelings around their sexuality," a girls' phys ed teacher at Brockton High School told me. It seems they were most interested in relationships, questions such as: How do you know when a boy loves you? or How can you trust a boy? Adolescence is a most difficult time, and they need support to understand feelings and sense the consequences of what they do. It is a time when moral questions loom large, so that the impact of the school — being the agency giving the advice — is crucially important.

Sex educators simply cannot ignore the questions of morality, even though they may want to focus on a deeper understanding of the human emotions and relationships that are involved in the sex act. But sooner or later the questions of what's right and what's wrong, or what's permitted and what's not, begin to crop up. Peter Robertson, the former Toronto board consultant, now a professor at the

College of Education, says educators may as well realize "that moral questions will be uppermost in the kids' minds, and there's no way you can overlook it." Some handle these questions in a rather mechanical way. "I don't moralize, I stay right away from that," one phys ed teacher told me. "How do I avoid it? I tell them what different people say. I explain the seven methods of birth control, but we spend a good deal of time on the rhythm method. And I explain what the church says about it, and then I say it's up to you."

Others take a more personal tack, trying to explore the meaning of morality. One favorite technique is to stage a debate among three members of the class, one taking a hard-line puritan's position, another taking a totally permissive stance, and a third arguing for the stituational ethic. It is sure to be a shocker for some of the students, and old hat for some. At any rate, says Robertson, "whether we teach anything there or not, the school is the social milieu where the morality of the home will be challenged by the larger society. Sex education is recognizing that. The kids are growing up, they're growing breasts and they're growing feelings toward the opposite sex, so the health teacher says, 'Let's talk about that.'"

And what then? Clive Beck at the department of history at the Ontario Institute for Studies in Education, proposes that schools strive for "a post-conformity, autonomous approach to morality." By this he means building a moral sense on a deep understanding of human needs and desires, and of how these can best be fulfilled through the institutions of society. This entails a fresh new look at the family, the school, and society at large, and would present a major challenge to the chauvinism and authoritarianism so prevalent in the school culture.

Particularly relevant is the issue of women's rights. It so

happens that sex education takes place in a department that is not completely home free when it comes to sexist discrimination. Pat Kincaid did a study of this problem herself, in which she revealed that the system provided less than half as much money to girls' phys ed ($8,695) than to boys' phys ed ($22,230) in the 1972-73 school year at 12 major secondary schools. (Boys' enrollment was 9,978, girls' 8,867). She also pointed out the grossly biased distributions of awards at the co-educational track meet held at the Canadian National Exhibition in May 1973, in which boy winners received medals and trophies while girl winners received crests and ribbons. There was an outcry about this, so in June the board resolved that equal awards must be presented in future.

One audio-visual making the rounds of sex classes is *Anything You Want To Be,* a 15-minute film by a school girl, Liane Brandon. She runs for student council president and ends up being a secretary. She majors in chemistry and finds her beakers changing into baby bottles. "I think I want to be a woman, whatever that is," she comments, and ends the film after a forced change from graduate to housewife, with a piercing scream. "Everything that's in that film exists in every school system in Ontario, I'm sure," Robertson commented. In physical education, there was the grossly distorted emphasis on male sports, to a point where new girls' vocational schools had been built without swim pools or playing fields, while boys' schools had both. Such disparities a good sex education course would have to explain, somehow or other.

The Task Force on Women's Rights, set up in 1972 to redress the wrongs, got at the root problems in its November 1972 conference entitled "A New Look at the Socialization of Children in the School System". The problem had to do with deeper structural faults than the oppression of women alone. As Lester Kirkendall points out, simply to resolve the double standard could result in "a single standard with exploitation appearing in a different guise, but as hurtful as ever." Yet by 1974 little had changed, and it remained questionable whether the system could remedy the more conspicuous forms of chauvinism, much less deal with the underlying causes.

It is almost a truism that to teach morality, an institution needs to clean its own house. The conventional texts on family life education point this out in relation to the family, as in this snippet from the Grade 11 text, *Families:* "Parents who tell the child what is right, but themselves do what is wrong, are poor examples for a bewildered child." And Gloria Torrance, who was in the midst of writing a new guideline on marriage, observed the truth of it. "How they treat one another, man and wife, really has a greater bearing on a child's sexuality than anything that's done in terms of teaching in a school situation. The marriage guide I'm working on is to help them see that how they relate, how they see each other, is what sex education is all about."

The same applies to the school. Its role is still less central to child development than the home, yet it becomes more crucial as it delves into the education "of the whole child," as the progressive motto would have it. How a school teaches sex education — or anything else, for that matter — is a moral act. And the fact that sexuality has to do in large part with the flow of communication makes it hard to teach with any kind of moral fidelity in a harsh, authoritarian setting.

When Clive Beck wrote the booklet, *Moral Education in the Schools*, he was not wildly optimistic about the prospects of a truly moral education. "I do not think we are aware of the tremendous backlog of authoritarianism toward younger people . . . that exists in our society," he wrote. "It pervades our school systems, our family arrangements, our laws, our whole society. The inferior status of women in our society, barbaric though it is, is easily outweighed by the disrespect and subservience to which we commit our children."

To bring moral education into the school would require a recasting of the format. The sex education teachers try, but against great odds. Michaluk's class at Humberside, which sits on the floor in the old cafeteria, gives it an earnest try. As he told me, "In my classes the students are quite as free as they want to be." Are they inhibited? I asked. "Very, I find them very inhibited. It doesn't have to be just about sexuality, it can just be about emotions and feelings. They lack the skills — even the vocabulary — to talk about some of these things." Does the rotating schedule encourage inhibition? "Yes, I get that from the students themselves. When things just bog down and I finally stop and point that out, they will say, 'I don't even know him and him and her, and I'm not going to talk about all these things.'"

Taken seriously, sex education forced the educators to dissolve the old authoritarian approaches inside the classroom. It wouldn't work to teach sex only from the lectern. The sex educators had the presence to see that authoritarian structures were anathema to sexuality, that to preserve the old controls taught just the opposite of what sex was all about. Theodore Roszak in *The Making of the Counter Culture* spoke of the dynamic effects of sexuality in authoritarian structures: "To liberate sexuality would be to create a society in which technocratic discipline would be impossible. But to thwart sexuality outright would create a widespread, explosive resentment that required constant policing . . ."[5] So at least in their curriculum guides, and to some degree in their method, they drew on a new human sensitivity. Students were to sit on mats and

[5] Page 14.

feel the rhythms of the body, the breath, the heartbeat. This gave them a feel for themselves, and as they began to level with their peers they began to explore new areas of human life. The key was "climate setting" at which one third of the class time was properly spent. "If we did a good job with this, we wouldn't need to worry about whether we got the content across," Gloria Torrance said. "That would just follow."

I asked Pat Kincaid if the newly personalized approach of sex education was spilling over into other areas. I struck a sore spot. "I don't think many teachers know what's going on," she said. "It's really compartmentalized. We just don't have the time to look around. . . . In the seven years I've been here I can remember three times I sat down with someone in another department to talk about what we were offering, and that was because of an overlap." She also found it difficult to sustain the open communication sometimes achieved in the health program. "We tend to forget about it in other things. You're expecting them to be open and honest in that particular unit, and you close them off when you're in basketball — you defeat the whole purpose."

Sex educators in Toronto plowed fertile ground, but they did it in one small acre of the educational kingdom. "It's an open question," Gloria Torrance told me in an aside, "whether we can teach any of this stuff in that setting." She was referring to the traditional authoritarian structure. It was an aside; her main message was: Yes we can. It was mysterious how the asides seemed so formidable, yet so dismissable. The asides seemed a preface to what had to be done, an admission once verbalized, easily and soon forgotten. "I think I see a trend toward humanizing," Gloria Torrance was saying. "I think people are more conscious of the ways they relate to other people." It seemed faintly possible in sex education. The signs I saw in the whole institution did not convince me. With the trend toward personal openness, one could not deny the trend toward subtler controls. Without great care, once the luster had faded sex education would succumb to the larger mechanics of schooling.

To make sense of it? That is for the youth to do, and the sense consists of a head full of information and skills, assembled in dribs and drabs, crammed at exam time and distilled into handwritten essays, which will get a man into university, into a good job, and, with luck, happily married. Sex education is part of the collage, one more splotch on the canvas. Sex finally became a high school subject in its own right — and much like any other, a fully accredited three-week sequence of 40 minutes a day, another thing to go to and get graded for. It was a valiant try, but in the end it made hardly a dent in the crusty requisites of high schooling. That last frontier kept its bounds to fit nicely into the routine — sex ed from 9:10 to 9:50, mathematics from 9:55 to 10:35, sociology from 10:40 to 11:20, and so on. Sex ed was part of phys ed, which made up one credit a year, and it takes 36 credits to earn a high school diploma. And it's easy. Nobody fails phys ed.

It didn't seem to me to be a good sign that Peter Robertson was the first to get transferred out when the 1970 budget crackdown came. He had written the greater part of four guidelines, including *Human Sexuality* and *Human Relations*, (though the bureaucracy had refused him a byline) and had lobbied for it until the hierarchy finally approved and published it. He was gone, Gloria Torrance was carrying on, and Robert Gladish was being philosophical about his dwindling department: "I don't look at it as all that bad, if I did I'd go crazy I guess, trying to build political power here to preserve the existing services." And so the impetus dwindles, having carved out an enclave, but scarcely touched the system. "But I don't know what else we can do but work on it little by little," John Michaluk told me. "That's some theme song, little by little, but I don't know how else we'll do it."

Chapter 7

WHAT IT COSTS

The cold truth dawned like a winter sun in 1970. The happy spring-like euphoria of the early 1960's had mellowed into late 1960's flowers-and-liberation. The Hall-Dennis Report had bloomed a few brief seasons, the elementary schools were "freed up", the high schools were offered free options. But in 1970, the Big Cutback came. The forces of austerity would get education for having been the spoilt child of the 1960's.

The Economic Council of Canada in 1962 had called education the nation's best long-term investment. Now it advised restraint. The pay-off seemed nonexistent, now that the economy was in a slump and education costs had far exceeded the 8.5 per cent annual increase the ECC had predicted. A survey of 360 high schools led the council to see that family factors had more to do with student performance anyway than elaborate equipment and teacher quality or quantity. "Our secondary school systems may, in general, have reached a certain level of maturity in which significant improvements in the performance or aspirations of students may *not* be best obtained by further buildup of resources."

The economy had spoken. The school system would respond.

But it was quite a reversal. In 1968, as far as Education Minister William Davis had been concerned, "education for years to come has to be the No. 1 priority in government spending", *Globe and Mail* reporter Kenneth Smith reported. These words were only slightly less reassuring than those Davis used in 1963, when he spoke on "Our Booming School System: Can We Pay For It?" to the Rotary Club of Toronto. "Even the financial burden, admittedly staggering as it is, is well within our power to carry without more than slowing somewhat the giant strides we are making in all other aspects of our economy," he reassured. "We must view these coming events in the proper perspective. Part of this requires that we put first the things of real and lasting worth, which to me means giving top priority to education during at least the next two decades."

The next two decades? Seven years later, having just established the new county boards that January, Davis in September called the new trustees and directors together and talked tough. This is how John Kelsey of *The Globe and Mail* reported it: "Smooth Bill Davis, the minister of education, calmly stood in front of 400 school board chairmen and directors of education yesterday afternoon and told them to stop making stupid mistakes."

It was the first time since amalgamation that Davis had met the local leaders. He used it to make them a public example. When a man from the Simcoe County board asked him to spare the counties the tax hardships of the previous spring, Davis shot back: "If you can assure me that all the budgets from all over Ontario are no bigger than they need to be, then there'll be no problems, but it is a two-way street." He warned them to "put your own house in order, or the pressure will mount for the department to do it for you." Davis was flanked by Premier John Robarts and Treasurer Robert Welch, and their message was simple: "They set forth, in stark terms, a program of fiscal retrenchment," recalled William McCordic, Metro Toronto's education director. Welch hammered home the point by telling the educators that if the spending trends kept on "by the year 2000 the entire gross national product of Canada would have to be spent on education. . . . We cannot permit these projections to happen."

Silly as it was, that sounded alarming. It was designed to sound alarming. The province was ready to act. It began to wield the big stick by quietly sending through the Legislature Bill 228, a 23-word amendment to the Department of Education Act that gave the minister power to issue orders governing expenditures "that may be made by a board for any purpose." Ministry officials assured local educators that it didn't matter; Davis had that power already, and anyway he didn't intend to use it. McCordic commented sagely, "the minister is just making sure his musket is dry", and most directors throughout the province, alerted by a warning notice in the 1969 Ministerial estimates, suspected a crackdown.[1] "It left a bad taste in the mouths of the trustees generally," John Darling told me in 1970, when he was chairman of Waterloo County Board of Education. "I'm elected to handle the educational affairs of this municipality, and all of a sudden Big Brother knows best." But there was little to be done about it; the bill slipped through the House in 11 days, becoming law on December 2, 1969.

That was the buildup. In October, 1970, came the clincher. Davis sent the grant announcements for 1971 to the school boards with a letter saying the Big Squeeze had come. "I cannot emphasize too strongly," Davis wrote, "the need for every possible economy in the light of the

[1] The notice read: "If local authorities, because of their limited jurisdiction, should find it difficult to implement fiscal policies which are in line with provincial priorities, they would be required to revise their fiscal requirements according to norms which would be formulated by the Department."

economic pressures which prevail at the present time." Then he announced what seemed to be absolute limits on the amount they could spend in 1971. Faced by a different set of forces, Davis had little yen "to put first the things of real and lasting worth" as he had advised the Rotarians. His action, dictated by the Treasury Board of Cabinet, marked the first time Ontario's central government had set absolute limits on school board spending.

Prior to this, the province had set a limit on the amount on which it would contribute grants, but if any board wanted to spend more than that it could do so out of local taxes. The new edict pegged spending at a provincial maximum of $545 an elementary pupil and $1,060 a secondary student. Each year the province would re-adjust the spending level. Areas such as Metro Toronto, which far exceeded this amount, would be given two years to bring their spending down to the provincial norm. (The province later padded it out with a great variety of urban "weighting factors", stretched the two-year deadline to three years, provided a major advance on credit, and in other ways eased the shock. At the moment, though, it looked fierce.)

It took months before what happened began to sink in. To be sure, the Metro Toronto trustees had been toying with restraints of their own. At one briefing session executive director William McCordic lectured them on the perils of overspending. He gave them a graph to show them those skyrocketing costs, and they resolved to do better.[2] In the past, they had budgeted from bottom up, they started with the educational needs at hand, and after modest trimming by the Metro board, they simply set the tax rate accordingly, after deducting the amount the province would provide in grants. And the tax rate always went up. During the

[2] See the graph on next page. At that point it reached only to 1970. Subsequent spending restrictions slowed the rate of increase, but did not stop rising costs.

WHAT IT COSTS

THE METROPOLITAN TORONTO SCHOOL BOARD

PERCENTAGE INCREASES OVER 1965 IN:
- Gross Expenditures and Ceiling Limitations _____ A
- Mill Rate _____ B
- Taxable Assessment _____ C
- Enrolment _____ D

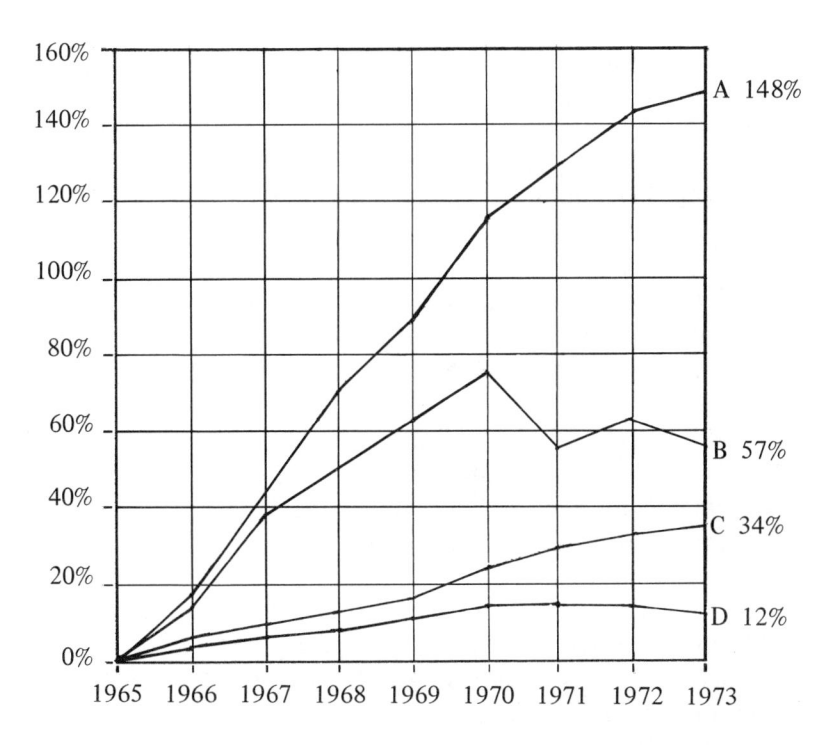

A 148%
B 57%
C 34%
D 12%

June 17, 1974

1960's the increases averaged $25 a year for an average Metro Toronto home. Everybody felt a little guilty about that, but nobody knew how to stop it. McCordic thought it was about time they started what he called "top-down budgeting". This meant they would set a maximum budget figure, and then restrict the educational programs to fit it. Some trustees were bottom-uppers, others were top-downers, and nobody knew just how to resolve it. I remember Reginald Stackhouse, a trustee for Scarborough, telling me he was a top-downer, but by the time the crunch came he had himself a seat in Parliament for Scarborough East.

At any rate, the trustees didn't have to decide. Davis and the Treasury Board did it for them. By the time they got around to the next year's budget, Davis' curtailment was in force. The Metro board had the top-down joy of wringing $13-million from its flat budget of $364-million in 1971.

The Ontario populace seemed to demand a cutback in spending. When Davis ran for the premiership in February 1971, he was hotly challenged by educational hard-liner Allan Lawrence, then the justice minister, who wanted to reduce education far more abruptly than Davis had done. Davis slipped into the premier's office by a mere 44-delegate margin at that Progressive Conservative convention. He called an election for that October, an election that could have been a testing ground for the restrictions. The issue was muddied by Davis' eleventh-hour rejection of tax support for Catholic high schools, bringing any wayward vestiges of Orange Ontario back to the Conservative fold, but the public's approval of the education restrictions seemed validated as well when the Conservatives came back strongly vindicated, and even the educators grudgingly agreed that most people seemed to feel education costs had to be curbed. It seemed that the only public body that failed to get this message was the Toronto Board of Education.

It had mystified me how the local trustees could be so

WHAT IT COSTS 139

oblivious to the pressures they were supposed to be feeling about school costs. They were the ones who should have known; they didn't feel it. They fought the 1969 election with little awareness of general overspending. The big issues were community access to the schools, more openness in board affairs, and responsible business operations. The public had been stung by reports of Hawaiian junkets and lavish farewell banquets, but these were seen as flukes, not as examples. The onus was on better bookkeeping, not so much on cutting back. A group calling itself the Interested Parents in Ward 10 and 11 summed up the general discontent this way: "We believe that the present Board of Education, with the exception of Dr. Lister and Mr. Lowes, is grossly incompetent. It has not provided leadership. It has concerned itself with trivia, failed to deal imaginatively and intelligently with major issues in education, and has been unable or unwilling to communicate with parents and students."

All of it true. But it was not the fiscal scalding one might have expected from the part of the city paying the biggest residential tax bills.

I began to see that overspending had become a provincial issue before it became a local issue. It was a major concern to the provincial Conservatives, whose Big Blue Machine swept them to yet another victory in 1971 with the aid of an estimated $5-million in donations from unnamed private and corporate sources. But to the local community, which got the benefit from the previous decade's extensive outlay for education, the complaints were hardly heard. It was, after all, the big corporations that were hardest hit, even by the lowly property tax. The Toronto Dominion Bank, for example, had to pay a school property tax of $2.3-million in 1972 for only its two towers in the Toronto Dominion Centre, while an average homeowner paid out $500. The relative impact of these two taxpayers on the government is hardly equal. The teachers were quite right in pointing out that, in our industrial democracy, "public opinion is what politicians perceive to be the opinion of *significant* groups of the public."[3]

This is not to say that rising school costs went totally unnoticed in local property tax bills. A man with a $40,000 house in Toronto saw his property tax rise an average of $25 a year during the 1960's, to a point where he paid $510 in 1972. His education tax bill had doubled during the decade, while the municipal property tax (for sewers, street lighting, and other city government functions) had increased by two-thirds. In 1970, for the first time in many years, the education tax was actually higher than the municipal tax.

Costs were going up for many reasons. Studies done by the Ontario Secondary School Teachers Federation showed that education costs per pupil increased by 93 per cent from 1961 to 1968. Roughly one third of the increase was caused by simple inflation. The rest went into an expanded system. The total school population rise during the 1960's alone would have meant a rise of nearly 50 per cent in elementary costs and a 100 per cent rise in secondary costs.[4] But the most costly single improvement was a decrease in the student-staff ratio. In 1960, there were 30 pupils to each elementary teacher; in 1969 there were 25. In 1960, there were 23 students to a secondary school teacher; in 1969 there were 16. The classes grew smaller. But do not be fooled. Many of these teachers were not classroom teachers; they were principals, counsellors, consultants, vice-principals. Figures on actual class sizes were not kept,

---

[3] *Financing Public Education in Ontario: the 1970's*, the Ontario Secondary School Teachers' Federation, 1973, p.XXV. Italics theirs.

[4] *Financing Public Education in Ontario 1970*, Ontario Secondary School Teachers' Federation, Toronto, 1971, p.13.

but it is instructive to know that the number of certified personnel at the schools who actually taught in classrooms fell from 78 per cent in 1962 to 68 per cent in 1972 throughout the province.[5]

School services as well were obviously expanding. Classes for slow learners and perceptually handicapped multiplied. Teachers became available for remedial reading. Speech therapists sprang up. Specialists for music, physical education, and French began to tour the schools. Schooling expanded to take children at the age of 4 instead of 5: junior kindergarten came into vogue. At high school, occupational courses opened. Technical classes became widely available. Teachers gained a free period, in addition to lunch, to prepare lessons or grade papers; they acquired decent wages. Teams of psychiatrists, psychologists and counsellors came on staff. Swim pools became standard equipment in new schools. A New Canadian program worth $4-million a year was added in Toronto.

With all this, there just wasn't much protest at the local level against overspending. Thus you had Robert Orr, a Conservative trustee representing strongly lower middle-class Ward 3, telling the board in a budget debate: "I go through the ward and I talk to people about this, and I haven't any real complaint from people regarding their taxes. So let's get this straight. It's the politicians that are telling us we can't have high taxes. It's not the *people* who are telling us that, at least they're not telling me that." And Herbert Barnes, the trustee who fought hardest in Toronto to cut spending, who advertised himself as the taxpayer's avenger, was turned out in the 1972 election in wealthy Ward 10. Later he said bitterly: "I don't think the public gives a damn about the money trustees spend. I spent three years on the board hammering away about saving, and was

---

[5] *Financing Public Education in Ontario: the 1970's,* the Ontario Secondary School Teachers' Federation, 1973.

defeated by 400 votes." In short, education costs weren't an issue locally until the central government decided to clamp down.

A closer look at the tax structure shows why trustees didn't feel the urgency. It is another element in the larger story of the centralized takeover. It warrants telling here because it shows how powerfully consoling the takeover became.

One of the truisms of public life is that the property tax is bad. It always had been a hard one to evade and a rough one to pay. It came due in big lump sums, unlike the low-key sales tax and the graduated income tax. Furthermore, it had a reputation for being notoriously regressive, soaking the poor disproportionately to the rich. During the 1960's Ontario farmers grumbled at being doubly hit. In addition to the tax on income, they paid the property tax on their chief source of income. Land inflation drove their assessments to a point where Gordon Hill, president of the Ontario Federation of Agriculture, documented cases of farmers paying an education tax of $650 while nearby doctors, lawyers and teachers were paying $230. Pensioners, too, were undercut. "It gets to the point where we have to sell our homes in order to pay our taxes," said Tom Smith, vice president of the United Senior Citizens of Toronto.

The government remedied these problems with a 25 per cent rebate to farmers and a tax credit system for home-owners, making the property tax less regressive.

Still the move was on to reduce its weight as an educational revenue. By 1960 the province had a whole arsenal of taxes that could be enlisted centrally for education — the personal income tax, the retail sales tax, the corporation tax, the gasoline tax, the succession duty, the Liquor Control Board of Ontario. Any one of them was less onerous to more people than the lump-sum property tax. "All taxation involves political pain of some degree so that politicians have a vested interest in making taxes seem invisible and relatively painless regardless of consequences for equity and efficiency," H.P. Moffatt and Wilfred Brown point out in their little book, *New Goals, New Paths*.[6] The province was eager to do what it could.

But the property tax had two old-fashioned virtues that none of the other taxes could match. It was highly *visible*, and it was obstinately *local*. The tax, for all its faults, had served the province for 130 years as a cornerstone of local school government. "We have been unable to discover or devise a workable alternative to the real property tax as a major revenue source of local governments which would not drastically reduce, or even destroy, either local autonomy or local fiscal responsibility." So wrote the Ontario Committee on Taxation, headed by Lancelot Smith in 1967.

The public body that spends money has to be accountable to the people who pay that money. Or, as the Smith Committee put it in economic jargon, "to avoid a misallocation of resources, local autonomy must be coupled with fiscal responsibility." Moffatt and Brown point out that the political pain of raising funds should fall at the same level of government that has the pleasure of spending them.

The fiscal coup d'etat began with George Drew's "50 per cent promise" in 1943. The central government would shoulder half the cost of schooling so that, as he put it, "the owning and improving of homes and farmlands, which are the very foundation of our society, will not be discouraged by excessive taxation." His Conservatives swept to power, and they kept their promise.

Twenty-six years later, having finally achieved the

---

[6] Published by the Canadian Teachers' Federation in June 1973. Page 116.

Drew promise in 1970, Davis promptly set a new goal of 60 per cent.[7]

The Metro School Board's own newsletter of February 1973 describes the province's new self-imposed quandary as if it had been inevitable: "In order to achieve this last goal (of 60 per cent support) the Province had to limit the total amount being spent: otherwise local boards simply took the larger grants and boosted their own share as well, leaving the proportion paid by the Province unchanged." It seemed straight-forward. But it was conventional hokum, widely bought as gospel truth by educationists throughout the province. Behind this apparent inevitability, something else had happened. The province, with ever so benevolent intentions, had undercut the mainstay of local government.

The danger of this had been spelled out quite clearly by the Ontario Committee on Taxation of 1967 (known as the Smith Report): "If local authority and fiscal responsibility are to be maintained, the property tax must remain the major tax source." And the Royal Commission on Education in Ontario (known as the Hope Commission), also had declared in 1950 that localities should bear the main responsibility for financing education: "We believe this is necessary to ensure any measure of real control."

Richard Thorman, Metro's school finance controller, pleaded the same cause in his brief to the province's Costs of Education Committee in March, 1972: "Although there must be a level of provincial equalization in the funding of local programs," he wrote, "there needs also to be a freedom of local choice demonstrated by the preparedness or otherwise of local taxpayers to fund programs to meet local needs. The cost control aspect of the local tax on real estate should not be underestimated."[8] The message had not been

---

[7] The Liberals and New Democrats chided the government for not going further, and at one point former Liberal leader John Wintermeyer proposed 100 per cent.

[8] "The Necessity, Implications and Nature of Cost Controls in Elemen-

hidden; it was only taken lightly as the central government sought to spur expansion beyond local tolerance. The school boards, for their part, seemed eager to sell their fiscal birthright for the benefits of larger and more specialized bureaucratic systems. The people, of course, were paying more taxes than ever before, but the taxes were harder to see. The portion labeled "education" went up at a rate nowhere near the rate of expansion of educational services.

By studying Toronto's tax rates over the decade from 1960 to 1970, I found that, had it not been for Queen's Park's increasing largesse, Toronto's public school system would have had to push property taxes 10 mills higher in 1970 than it did (or $104 on an average house). And 12 mills higher in 1972 than it did. This means quite simply that the local taxpayer did not feel the full brunt of growing education costs in his property tax. And the school trustees failed to get the message because, to all intents and purposes, they had stumbled into a bargain basement of educational goodies. They spent unwisely, but the responsibility could not be theirs alone. As the OSSTF observed without fully explaining why, "the relative easy money situation in which boards found themselves in the last half of the decade creates a climate friendly to innovation and change in the schools."[9] To say the least.

The province had eroded traditional restraints by doling out more money each year, and local administrators were only too glad to expand their jurisdictions with the ready cash. The provincial government had manoeuvered the school boards into the position of having to be throttled for having been overfed.

tary and Secondary Education to the Year 1980," the Metropolitan Toronto School Board, 1972, p.3.
[9] *Financing Public Education in Ontario 1970,* The Ontario Secondary School Teacher's Federation, p.51.

It was the inequity of the property tax that was made the occasion for the phasing out of local autonomy. Instead of major tax reform, the province chose centralized funding and control. But the property tax, in fact, is less regressive than many other taxes, and it can be reformed to cure its liabilities while preserving its strengths.[10] But its strengths, particularly its localism, had become a liability to the objectives of the province.

It should also be noted that much of the local school board's burden had been forced upon it by higher levels of government. For example, the Diefenbaker vocational-technical grant scheme boosted the number of shops and technical courses, while the province encouraged smaller classes and larger counselling staffs. Richard Thorman, Metro Toronto School Board controller of finance, contends that if the local school boards had been left to respond merely to local demands, their expenditures during the 1960's could have been far more modest. The burden the schools were asked to bear was increasingly centrally dictated, and for carrying out the new tasks, the province provided easy money —— until 1970.

In fact, it was built right in to the structure of the two-tiered Metro school system that local trustees would be inclined to spend all they could. It was the Metro board's responsibility to raise the local tax dollar, while it was the local boards' responsibility to expand the system, and thereby hung the problem. William McCordic, a founder of

[10] Two young researchers at the Massachusetts Institute of Technology have challenged the whole notion that property taxes for education need to be regressive. "We show that once the entire tax system is taken into account, single family homes are not 'overtaxed', and that, if fairly administered, the property tax would not be regressive. If this is conceded, then the demand for reductions in the property tax amounts to little more than a demand for middle-class *tax relief*, pure and simple, which could equally well be accomplished by reductions in any other tax instrument." Page 62 of *The Public Interest*, Winter, 1973, in an article by George Peterson and Arthur Solomon.

the Metro system, himself warned in 1958 that since local boards no longer carried full responsibility for raising their own funds, they were in a very expansive mood. Now, instead of holding back and weighing wisely, they had to fight for all they could get from the Metro pie. This pushed expenditures up and up.

By 1970 the province had legitimate grounds for saying the cost of education could be reduced. Education rode high on the hog with so much easy money. Most of it went into expansion and improvement, but the spill-off resulted in such things as elaborate new education centres, dubious pleasure trips by trustees, and inordinate farewell parties. When Davis made his "Smooth Bill Davis" speech in September 1969, he alluded to the Minkler affair as "a case of trusteeship run amok."[11] With school populations peaking, it seemed doubtful the trustees could exert the leadership needed to bring the juggernaut to heel. Davis fostered the idea that school boards were incapable of the task.

The province alone was powerful enough — now that local control had been undermined — to enforce the cutbacks. It chose to do so in a way that held back chiefly the large urban centres; especially Metro Toronto, while allowing the regions to catch up in terms of actual dollars spent per pupil.

Toronto had been, for some good and some bad reasons, a high-spending board. Its school buildings were better built, its services richer and more diversified, its caretaker staffs more numerous, its teachers better paid, than in most other parts of the province. Even among the five boroughs in Metro Toronto, the city was a heavy spender. Thus in 1972, it cost an average of $975 per elementary child in Toronto, while it cost $600 in Orangeville or Peter-

---

[11] · That was the $74,000 farewell celebration for Fred Minkler, former director of education for North York.

borough. The overall Metro ceiling was $750. The province ostensibly set out to equalize these figures.

This action superseded the grant equalization scheme of 1969, which linked the education tax bill in each area to the ability to pay. Cities could no longer decide to spend more on education even by taxing themselves more heavily for it. The measure placed a uniformity of expenditure on local areas regardless of local needs. This suited the provincial slogan of equal educational opportunity, but it never was shown that the dollar figure was a just index of equity, and urban weighting factors soon replaced the earlier informal arrangements that allowed the cities to spend more. The true objective was centralized control.

The cutback came during a wave of disillusionment; the government gave monetary teeth to a widespread feeling of discontent, of having been let down. "Too much magic was expected of education," the secondary teachers declared in 1973. "The great boom in education is over. It ended in 1970."[12] Education no longer was the splendid deliverer. Davis sealed its fate by declaring it a non-growth industry; the media dropped its fascination with educational hardware and technique. In Toronto, the newspapers shifted their attention, as if on cue, to mass transit and city politics.

The cutbacks themselves do not look drastic compared to the truly enormous outlay required each year. It was a mere 3 per cent reduction from what Metro Toronto might have spent to keep all its programs going. The Metro Toronto School Board allots to the six federated boards roughly $390-million a year in operating funds alone, which is more than most provinces spend in a year. It receives roughly one third of this as a grant from the province; two thirds comes from the property tax. The crackdown had the effect of slashing $13-million in 1971, $7-million in 1972 and

[12] Report of the Educational Finance Committee to the Ontario Secondary School Teachers' Federation, 1973, pp. 6,7.

$11-million in 1973, from the preliminary budgets drafted each year by the administrators. The crackdown, as Education Minister Thomas Wells said so often, was not an actual reduction in the cash amount, but "some control over the rate at which educational expenditures increased."[13] So despite slashing, Metro school costs rose from $351-million in 1971 to $389-million in 1973.

By the time the budget cutbacks took their bite, Davis had moved to the premiership. It was left to Wells, a subsequent Minister, to assure the public that no harm would come to the quality of education. "These ceilings represent a level of expenditure that should enable a board to provide and maintain a high standard of quality," he assured the Ontario Secondary School Teachers. Since he did not define what he meant by quality, we are left with the hypothesis that the result of the Conservative Cabinet's crackdown was the kind of quality it wanted, at least in the broad sweep of things. Here I will list some of the more obvious side effects, which need not be read as wholly accidental. They lay implicit in the structure that controls the schools.

Younger schooling. One ironic spin-off of the budget crackdown was the dramatic expansion of the system. This is how it happened. Metro Toronto School Board officials discovered in 1972 that by taking in the 8,210 four-year-olds who were still without junior kindergartens, the grant from the province would automatically rise by $2.8-million in 1973. The grant formula decreed it. The actual cost of extending junior kindergartens to all would be just $2.5-million that year, so Metro Toronto stood to gain a $300,000 bonus for extending the system in this fashion.

---

[13] From remarks by Wells to District 15 of the Ontario Secondary School Teachers' Federation, at Convocation Hall, University of Toronto, Feb. 18, 1972.

Upper-class neighborhoods had been pressing for junior kindergartens for years, but it took the budget crackdown to make their dream come true. It happened that by 1971, educational theorists were starting to question the wisdom of early education. Plainly it was the desire for custodial care — not educational benefits — that provided one of the main motives for the demand for an earlier age of admission.[14] This did not trouble the trustees in the least. They approved the expansion virtually without debate. In Toronto, only 18 upper-middle-class schools still lacked junior kindergartens, so it was they who "benefited" by this expansion. They had not been serviced before on grounds that their parents could afford their own custodial services.

Enrollment pressure. One little-known fact of schooling is that one in 14 students in Metro dropped out during the 1971-72 school year. That's 9,213 dropouts, and a dropout rate 22 per cent higher than the previous year. In Toronto itself, the system lost 9.4 per cent of its students between September and April. This is the kind of thing that the freeing up of the option system under H.S. 1 was designed to avoid. As the secondary teachers noted, "the essential aim in the late 1960's in moving towards a credit system in high schools and in offering a wider variety of subjects was to increase this retention rate even more." This was greatly spurred by the ceiling, since for every secondary student lost in 1972, $1,282 had to be deducted from the spending ceiling. It meant in plain words that teachers who couldn't hold their students — those with the least popular courses — stood the highest likelihood of losing their jobs, since the system could not afford to carry them. Alan Skeoch, head of history at Parkdale Collegiate Institute, contends that

---

[14] *New Goals, New Paths*, by H.P. Moffatt and Wilfred Brown, Canadian Teachers' Federation, 1973, p.17.

"the various departments of each high school are now locked, many unknowingly, in a life or death struggle for survival. . . . Your department either sells itself to the students or it wastes away." Which may not be all bad, but one of the ways of holding students is to demand little of them. The spending ceiling adds the sort of pressure that creates cynicism, and in many schools students are held by being coddled.

Larger classes. One most worthwhile gain during the rich years of the 1960's was a steady reduction of the size of classes. The student-staff ratio fell from 30:1 to 25:1 at elementary schools, and from 23:1 to 16:1 in secondary schools from 1960 to 1970. To be sure, the additional staff was not all teachers. Many were consultants, vice principals, administrators, counsellors. Class sizes shrank at a far slower rate of speed, but shrink they did.

The budget restrictions reversed that trend. As the crackdown came, making classes larger was always a tantalizing prospect, for to raise the ratio by just one secondary student across Metro saved approximately $6.3-million. The trustees in 1973 increased the secondary ratio by 0.8, despite falling enrollments. Thanks only to hard-nosed teacher power, the 1972 levels were restored in 1974 at the secondary level. Nothing short of the threat of mass resignations forced the province to lay out the additional cash to make this possible, and even then Toronto cut its central staff by 15 per cent and reduced its maintenance program by $2.5-million to bring it off.

Metro rescued. The budget restrictions put such stress on Metro Toronto's two-level system that its collapse seemed possible. Wells came to the rescue of the Metro School Board in a subtle shift that also benefited Wells' home borough of Scarborough. (He represents Scarborough North.) The Metro board, for 21 years the fiscal arbiter for Toronto and the boroughs, was hotly maligned as the ceilings upset the gradual plan for fiscal equity, and put pressure on Toronto to cut its spending drastically to aid Scarborough, which lagged far behind. For example, Scarborough's average elementary pupil cost in 1971 was $647 compared to Toronto's $964. While the money had flowed freely, the "have not" boroughs could catch up without hurting the "haves", but now Toronto and North York were loath to split their depleted allowances to help a weaker brother.[15] Wells reacted by allowing all the cost of operating the Metro board ($1.5-million, including the cost of schools for the deaf and retarded) to be exempted from the ceiling, and in 1973 asked that one fourth of that amount be awarded to Scarborough. This helped save the Metro system which had served as an invaluable buffer between province and city.

Formulas imposed. School officials knew their one hope of avoiding conflict while slicing the Metro pie was to agree in advance on fiscal formulas. They worked them out in exhausting detail on staff, furniture, maintenance, aides, and even textbooks. So many of a certain kind of student meant so many of a certain kind of teacher. For example, 15.8 shop students resulted in one shop teacher in any school in Metro. At first designed as a tool to bring equity, they later seemed to Toronto trustees a weapon to impose conformity.[16] Toronto drew up a brief in February 1973 cal-

[15] Professors Tom Williams and David Wiles of the Ontario Institute for Studies in Education warned that this conflict, if continued into 1973, could be fatal to the Metro system. "Unless the equity question is resolved, forget Metro," Williams told a school trustees conference at the Four Seasons Sheraton Hotel in 1973. "Either someone is going to do it for you, or you are going to blow yourselves apart."

[16] The staff allocation committee of the Metro School Board mocked the complexity of the staffing formula in this sentence in a January 1974

ling the spending ceilings "dictatorial and arbitrary devices" that are "not acceptable in a democratic society."[17] As the formulas forced schools into rigid arrangements of hardware and personnel, the system suffered a blight of sameness. The right to discretionary levies, by which individual boards in the past had financed swim pools at their own behest, was cancelled. There were still province-wide weighting factors for special classes, inner-city schools, New Canadians, French classes — but these were rigidly imposed. "The ceiling formula approach is defensible," Thorman told the Committee on the Costs of Education, "only if society is prepared to accept the degree of homogenization of the education process which must accompany it."

Special ed expanded. Edward McKeown, chief inspector of special education in 1973, made a strong case for transferring the system's 69 reading clinic teachers from Donald Rutledge's Language Study Centre to his own Special Education Department. The shift to McKeown's department was rationalized to trustees as a better way of integrating things. McKeown gave them a report full of bureaucratic jargon ("can develop a co-ordinated approach while at the same time maintaining the flexibility to provide a continuum of programs to meet a variety of needs") on why this was so. The trustees bought it. But Rutledge said later the real issue was money. By shifting those 69 teachers, McKeown won for the Metro coffers a richer "weighting" of the provincial ceiling formula. This raised

report: "The present formula has as its basic characteristic a 'school by school' nature with the result that it takes considerable time to compute the staff for each school (let alone a Board) when one takes into account that there are nine outputs, 20 parameters and 27 calculations in the formula."

[17] Brief to the Committee on the Costs of Education, Toronto Board of Education, February 1973, p.11.

the ceiling by $497,194 in 1974, allowing Metro to spend that much more money by this simple transfer. It was the sort of logic Rutledge could not refute. Thus the province gave Metro Toronto a half-million-dollar bonus for expanding its special education empire.

In early June of 1973 the city editor at *The Globe and Mail* asked me to visit a high school to see if the budget cutbacks were having any effect. I chose to visit Oakwood Collegiate, a school of 1,400 students and 59 nationalities, situated on the Escarpment on St. Clair Avenue. I arrived one day when Principal Edward Gordon was out, but Elizabeth de Corneille, the head of English, helped me set up a schedule for visiting classes and teachers. There was a little schedule mixup, until science head Don Whitewood took me in tow. "I'm sorry about this shuffling around," Mrs de Corneille called after us, as Whitewood ran resistance for me down one busy hallway during a class break, "It's awfully hard . . . in a . . . regimented system. . . ." She was a tactful lady, well aware of how it all looked to an outsider, but trying hard to do a good job within the system. The English department, I was to learn later, took the hardest rub of all, losing its privileged status of five-period days, and each teacher gaining 20 per cent more students. "If I had to pinpoint a department where the morale was the lowest," Gordon told me, "it would be the English department."

But meanwhile, on to science. Don Whitewood, a loquacious Scot, marched me into a typical high school lab, the teacher's desk a messy jungle of beakers, plastic hoses, transformers, wires and books. "We don't get any help from the maintenance department even to wipe off desks," Whitewood muttered. He was up until 1 a.m. the night before grading 100 papers for Grade 11, he had to prepare next year's course outlines by June 18, all his Grade 13 marks were due that Friday (there were 110 in Grade 13), he had lessons to prepare and materials to get ready, and Whitewood wasn't feeling on top of things. "You're in a position," he told me, "where the left hand scratches the right ear all day . . . and it's just a drag, because you come in the morning and you're just beat, and it's no good because you keep chipping away at the kids. In spite of yourself, you keep chipping away at the kids. They don't deserve that."

We ran into science teacher John McEwan who told me that he was lucky to have just three "preparations" — other teachers have five. This meant his six classes a day were partly repeats, so he only needed to prepare three lessons. But that's still 190 students. To grade all their assignments would take three hours, just spending one minute on each paper. As he talked, they seemed to blur into digital non-entities. "I've lost a few bodies," he told me, "there were 200 at the beginning of the year."

He went into a storeroom and fetched a plastic tub of broken glassware. "They're relatively careful with glass, but —" he viewed the breakage ruefully. An object lesson. If one kid in each class broke one glass a week, that's seven to be replaced. A graduated cylinder costs $3.75; two dozen breakages would wipe out the entire supplies budget for Grade 9 science. I began to get the message.

Whitewood told me that's why students no longer do many experiments themselves. It's a luxury they can't afford. The simple experiment that shows the effects of water freezing in a bottle was once done in groups of four. "We can't afford the bottles to break them, so we're just doing it at the front for everybody to watch." This penny preoccupation went so far teachers were asking students to pay the 8 cents to mail report cards home to parents; eight times 1,000 is $80, enough for 26 graduated cylinders. Whitewood's supplies budget had been pinched to a point where he had 30 cents for each Grade 9 child. "We are getting to the point where the kids think we're really cheap," he said. "And we are."

Later, Principal Gordon agreed: "How do you blame the kids thinking it's Mickey Mouse when you see $29-million spent down there on Ontario Place and then they come to school and haven't even enough money to pay for the experiments?" And Frank Procopio, a Grade 10 student whose father is a chef and who wants to be a pharmacist, told me that to dissect a frog in biology, the students had to bring razor blades from home. They were down to one available worm for every two students, he said. "I was half expecting them to say, 'Bring your own grasshopper.' Everybody in the school brought 50 cents to buy science equipment. I mean, 50 cents isn't very much, but . . ."

"Where do all our parents' taxes go?" asked Italia, Grade 10, who wants to become a psychologist, and was listening in.

"Ontario Place, where else?" Frank replied.

Whitewood and I came into Tony Constantino's classroom. He teaches two levels of Grade 9 science and two levels of Grade 11 physics. How does he manage? "It's possible if you're willing to put in anywhere from four to six hours every evening, it's possible to give reasonable assignments. I have a feeling inside myself that I'm able to do that. But it's frustrating in this classroom with 37 kids, when you have to go around looking for chairs." The lab was built for 24.

All this is trivial in itself, but the undercurrent of cynicism spoke louder than words. Here were inmates and wardens, at once parasites and victims of the system, who having learned dependency in the good days of plenty, found themselves robbed when the good days were over. The sys-

What It Costs

tem seemingly taught nothing that would liberate them to seek solutions outside the old routines. Much later, when in November 1973 the teachers finally staged a work-to-rule protest, the students skipped school one day to march on Queen's Park. And Principal Gordon managed to set up an Oakwood Community School Council to advise and support him on budget matters. But the old routines of schooling would grind on.

It mattered a great deal to Wayne Dignard, a Grade 13 student and son of a railway worker, who failed chemistry that year at Oakwood. "I make my teachers work for a living, but during the work-to-rule, you just didn't want to ask them things." Will he make it into university? "I have a chance to get into a poor university," he said. "I'm trying Laurentian at Sudbury." The cutback was felt on morale as much as anything — classes for which there weren't desks, lack of paper towels, broken equipment. It made simply getting a decent education that much rougher, and in the process those on the border like Wayne were pushed back. Failed courses could be made up in the summer, but not for Wayne who had to get himself a job and was planning to join a section gang near Banff on the Canadian National Railway. He hoped to become a physical education teacher, but it wasn't going to be easy.

Whitewood told me how his staff builds its own electronic equipment to save money. "We hustle around for a lot of cheapy parts. Now and then we get old TV sets so we can use resistors, and here are some crystal diodes from a computer board I found down on Queen Street." Crystal diodes cost 25 cents apiece that way; they cost $10 each if ordered through the Board of Education. "So it's much easier," he told me, "to go down and get it yourself." I asked why he doesn't send his students out to buy the stuff. He replied: "The kids aren't sophisticated enough to go down there and know what they're scrounging around for." Doubtless such an activity couldn't be timetabled into 40-minute periods either. A pity, though, because that seemed an obvious way to transform the budget cut from a curse to a blessing. But as it was structured, his physics department had to absorb the reduction of supplies from $1,100 in 1970 to $850 in 1973 simply by cutting corners. It seemed the only way.

What was happening was a retreat over the ground gained during the fat years. "What it means," said Gordon, "is that we're back to textbook teaching. All your talk about student involvement becomes a farce. . . . On the one hand, we're told to individualize our timetabling and instruction. On the other hand, we're told to cut spending. The teachers are caught in the middle, so what do they do?"

What they do, said Larry Podmore, head of history, is revert to the old methods of "swallow and vomit". There was no longer time nor resources to allow the free ranging needed to fully absorb the curriculum material. Teachers took recourse in the easily graded multiple choice exam, the old textbook routine. "Three weeks ago," said Maurice Smith, head of modern languages, "we had a consultant come in here from the Ministry of Education. This person told us just how we could do things according to HS1.[18] It was all very well, but there's no hope we can ever do it. There's no money, and there's no time."

The cutback fiasco lay not so much in its effect on the ordinary teacher as in its overtaxing of the best. Of course, some teachers never put in those four hours a night, or gave up several evenings a week coaching rugby, basketball or

---

[18] Circular HS 1 is the guideline from the Ministry setting out the new philosophy of secondary education, including subject promotion, broad areas of study and individualized instruction.

wrestling. But those who did now got sufficient pressure to break them or turn them cynical. "Sometimes," said Whitewood, "I just throw up my hands and say 'To hell with it all.'" Those who took seriously their teaching, who bought the Ministry's words about individualized instruction and independent study, in short, the good teachers, got the shaft. It paid not to care that much.

And the students? The poor, the non-Anglo-Saxon were plainly hurt the most. Oakwood excelled in vocal music, and it had a first-rate drama section. These two courses were the route to the outside world for many a home-bound, tradition-clad Italian youth. Music and drama offered the self-realization to make it possible. "In theatre arts this year there's 33 people and it's too big," Sarah, Grade 10, told me. "Theatre arts is individual instruction and you just have to have smaller classes." But the classes grew from 25 to 35 in the three years of the cutback, along with fewer props and less teacher time. In English, too, where lack of familiarity puts immigrants at a stark disadvantage, the lack of personal attention hurt the poor. Principal Gordon was blunt about it: "The cutbacks must take into consideration the cultural needs of the community, but by and large they don't. It's a middle class society we live in, and the kids at Oakwood are not going to be able to compete in that society with the cutbacks. The budget restrictions are a threat to the working-class immigrant kid. And that's the kid we're dealing with. He's the kid that's getting screwed. Morty Shulman's kids will do all right."

Chapter 8

THE SCHOOL BUREAUCRACY

Brother (age 9): The teachers get in trouble by the principal sometimes.
Sister (age 6): Yeah, if they're scolding the children too much.
Brother: No, if they're too rough with the children.
Sister: Yeah, that's what I meant by scolding too much.
Brother: Even the principal gets in trouble by the school board. And the school board gets in trouble by the government. And I don't know what the government gets in trouble by.
Sister: Maybe Queen Elizabeth.
Brother: Yeah. And Queen Elizabeth gets in trouble by God.

Working uphill, you pedal northward on McCaul Street toward an ancient red-brick Mining Building that baffles the north wind and creates a sudden breathless space. You pedal effortlessly onto College, turn right past a row of nine tightly pruned Chinese elms that line the Education Centre,

The School Bureaucracy

and you are at the doors of the establishment. The doors are glass and stainless steel. They are automated; they hum and swing open at the slightest touch.

Inside, to your right, an inquiry office. It was enlarged in 1972 to make room for the surveillance system. Wires lead out of here to 31 of the city's public schools. Somebody tampers with the side door at Montrose Public School, a red light flashes, a buzzer sounds, and caretaker Frank Dockrill dials 361-1111. A police cruiser is on the way. Harry Facey, comptroller of buildings, believes this system and the installation of unbreakable glazing materials helped reduce school vandalism in 1973 by 6 per cent — to a loss of only $630,150.

The surveillance panel is not readily visible to a visitor standing in the creamy marble foyer. He sees an orange shag rug with stainless steel-and-leather couches, and a large sgraffito mural depicting, as the tour guides used to say, "man's progress from his beginnings to his present relatively advanced state." Inscribed on the left wall are the names of all the past chairmen of the board, and all the past chief officials. An entranceway leads to Student Services, clearing station for social workers, attendance personnel, psychologists and psychiatrists. Three elevator shafts offer passage to six more floors of offices and a large auditorium.

The late Z.S. Phimister dreamed of making this edifice into a service centre. "Just as the blood flows through the heart . . . so the 3,300 teachers who face 90,000 pupils in 110 schools . . . will flow through this heart of the school system," he said, laying the cornerstone. But in the 14 years since it opened, dispersal came into vogue. Consultants moved out to the schools, superintendents established branch offices, and teachers complained at having to drive downtown in 4 p.m. traffic. Its staff decreased from 711 to 635 in 1973, as budget cuts took their toll. It is hardly the heart of the system; it is more backbone and cerebellum, the bureaucratic nerve centre to control its far-flung hands and feet.

The place is so clean it smells of SaniFlush and floor wax. Blue-clad caretakers seem always on the prowl; its public spaces are commodious but harshly angular. The second floor provides relief with pastel carpets and walls of dark walnut. It is the executive suite, and nothing is more sumptuous than the office of the Board chairman, with light green broadloom, beige walls and walnut trim, and a fully equipped washroom and shower.

Third floor houses an IBM 360 System Model 30 with 64K of core memory linked to input terminals in the schools, and offices of the Metro Toronto School Board. The other floors are given to cubicles for consultants and subject directors, each differing in tone and color by the tastes of the man or woman in charge. French director Robert Sweet's territory has racks of *L'Express* and *Le Macleans;* the Language Study Centre tends toward intellectual fare with *Encounter* and racks of paperbacks, both egghead and camp, from Nevil Shute's *On The Beach* to *Screwball* by Alta Armer; W. Winston Bates' maths quarters has the deflated look of a once-glorious New Math workshop gone flat; Margaret Wettlaufer's kindergarten seminar room has shelves of toys behind glass. And down the hall in Music, you can still get a recording of the 79th Annual Festival Concerts of 1965. In the physical education department are hardwood floors — it used to be a model gymnasium — occupied by tables, desks, projectors. A tiny closet holds large cases of family life materials — the "more confidential things" — consultant Gloria Torrance confides.

Still there's more. Joseph Sterioff, director of New Canadian programs, is housed on the fourth floor next to Facey's staff of draftsmen, architects and engineers. Teaching aids, tucked away on the fifth, is complete with television studio and control room, film library and miscellaneous hardware. Seventh floor has a frontal lobe known as the research department, headed by Dr Edgar Wright, and a once-grand library that under Leonard Frieser used to shake out Xerox copies on almost any subject on demand, even for school children (those days are past). And down in the basement is parking space for 54 cars and a small, fireproof door marked Dead File Storage, the resting place for old minutes when they die.

Down on first floor you step into an anteroom to the left, into the make-rich opulence of a Holiday Inn along the 401. Light fixtures that look like 12 brass candlesticks mark the entrance to the Board Room. Those swinging doors, padded with leather, hinged on brass, are sound proof. Inside is a rectangular horseshoe table, two dozen swivel chairs along its outer edge, and a raised podium at the open end for the chairman. The board's emblem hangs above his or her head. "Notice," says the tour guide pamphlet, "the pleasant colouring of the furniture and the raised paneling and draperies are well suited to the dignity and importance of the Board."

There are 25 public school trustees in the City of Toronto. Each of the city's eleven wards elects two, and three are elected separately by Roman Catholic school supporters. In the past, these persons have been assumed to be the governors of public education, directing school affairs at their tri-weekly meetings in their walnut-paneled chamber.

In fact, they function in a system that towers high above them through a hierarchy of civil servants, who answer, finally, to the Minister of Education. And he, in turn, to the provincial Cabinet. And that, in turn, to the voters of Ontario and the vested interests that help it maintain a majority in the Legislature at Queen's Park, which is just around a corner from the walnut-paneled chamber at 155 College Street.

The education system of Ontario reaches from the twenty-second floor of the Mowat Block, a steel, glass and concrete tower at Queen's Park, to as far away as Kakabeka Falls where Mrs Tine Parker teaches 21 pupils in one-room Hymers Public School. Between these points a vast interlocking bureaucracy monitors and controls the education enterprise.

The administrative elite in public schooling holds more discretionary power than any other civil service in Canada, political scientist Frank MacKinnon declared in his book *The Politics of Education*. He argued in 1960, before the expansions of the past decade, that no non-elected group ought to hold that kind of power. "Even if all of them had the highest qualifications, the arrangement would be dangerous, for no one man, group, or school of thought can exercise such power without eventually resorting to dogma, domination, and intolerance of criticism."[1]

How the bureaucracy assumed so much power over education is the subject of a book by Michael Katz, a historian at the Ontario Institute for Studies in Education, who also did a historical profile of the Hamilton school board. He points out that bureaucracies arose; they did not just happen for lack of other possibilities. During the late 1800's, North American society cast its schools in the bureaucratic mold in order to impress upon the upcoming generation the values of industrial capitalism. "Bureaucracy is not a neutral form; it represents the crystallization of

---

[1] He makes this statement on page 33 in a chapter on educational administrators which he titles, "Back-Seat Drivers". He also quotes another scholar, Frank Underhill who wrote in 1954: "What is really wrong with our Canadian school system is . . . its domination by interlocking directorates of orthodox bureaucrats in the provincial departments of education and exponents of orthodox doctrine in the colleges of education. . . . What is wrong with it is that it is laid down from above as the authoritarian party line. What most needs to be attacked is not the philosophy of these men but their power."

The School Bureaucracy

particular social values," he noted.[2] Whatever the values that shaped it then, the bureaucracy serves them still, and to understand what it teaches we have to know how it works.

At the fulcrum stands the Director of Education. He traditionally evokes the same inward snap of the heels as a general does in the Canadian Armed Forces, though more recently that severity has been displaced by the easy charm of a corporation executive. Humility only exalts the office; as the styles shift, the power continues to speak. "Administrative power is like spiritual power," explained John Turner, director of education in Peel County, "the more you share the more remains with you."[3] Whereas Toronto City Council has 15 department heads — housing, planning, works, and so on — each of them answerable separately to the council or the mayor, the school board invests supreme authority over the bureaucracy in one man. He wields control down through the hierarchical ranks, reconciling its many interests in his one powerful office. He traditionally signs his name to all reports, he approves all staff changes, he regulates all public pronouncements. The image of the office depends to some degree on the personality of the man. Graham Gore (1965-70) was a quiet, behind-the-scenes man, Ronald Jones (1970-73) was an apologetic liberal, and Duncan Green, the current director, is characterized by candor and disarming openness.

Contrary to popular opinion, directors are not the creatures of the Board of Education. The school board may hire its top officials, set their salaries, and place demands on their time. But its control is limited. A director's other loy-

---

[2] *Class, Bureaucracy, and Schools,* Praeger Publishers, 1971, page 6. See also pages 28 to 35. Katz later extended this analysis to the Canadian setting in the Fall 1972 issue of the *Canadian Forum.*
[3] *The Education Courier,* June 1971, page. 12.

alty is the Ministry. The in-house publications at the Ministry sometimes refer to directors as "agents of the Minister". Their duties are largely defined by the Education Act, and whatever local boards ask of them they must harmonize with their role as emissaries of higher authority. In fact, the top officials of any public school board in Ontario cannot be hired nor fired without the consent of the Minister of Education.

Regulations set by the provincial Cabinet ensure a narrow range of choice of school officials. Only those need apply who have worked their way up the educational hierarchy. Those who finally reach the top have most likely proved their talents in the teacher federations, become vice-principals or department heads, moved into consultant positions, then to principal, then to assistant superintendent, then to superintendent, then to assistant director, then to director. Ronald Jones could say he had spent 33 years in the Metro Toronto system by the time he became Toronto's director in 1970. Three years later he had reached retirement.

There are no shortcuts. A director must hold a superintendent's certificate, and to get that he must be a principal, and to become a principal he must be selected by the Ministry to take the six-week Principal's Course. Teachers stand in line for that Principal's Course. The bureaucracy chooses from among the ranks; Toronto sends a list of names each year to the Ministry. The Ministry selects fifteen.

So tight are the ties of administrators to Ministry that school boards often find themselves stymied. Their job becomes one of second-guessing the Minister, as Toronto did in its hassle over ethnic language classes.[4] In that game the administrators hold the balance of power, being the ones to speak to both sides and work out the compromises, usually

[4] See Chapter 2.

in advance of the Board making up its mind. In ways such as these the administration holds a grip on the activities of its so-called policy makers. That is how the decisions are tailored to the needs of the bureaucracy, within the larger logic of the political economy. David Wiles and Thomas Williams predict that professional domination will continue as long as the governing system keeps its present form. "In other words," they conclude in a paper for the May 1972 conference on school politics, "the political realities of current educational policy-making give the professionals an increasing control of decision making."[5]

MacKinnon's warning is 14 years old. Events since that time have made it no less true. As we explore the methods and mindset of the bureaucracy we can sense the impact it must have on the children in its care.

It was that crusty conservative, former Trustee Herbert Barnes, while representing Ward 10, who once made the comment that trustees seemed to be "the loyal opposition" while the school bureaucracy formed "the government". The description was apt, although the opposition seemed destined never to come to power. Trustees confronted by administrative power had a fairly simple choice. They could join the establishment and wield its token reforms, much as John Strachan, who wielded the axe for Upper Canada's family compact, or they could cast their lot with the loyal opposition, much on the order of Jesse Ketchum.

One good example of Establishment service comes from Barry Lowes, erstwhile chairman of both the Metro Toronto School Board and the Toronto Board of Education, who carried the pike for the bureaucracy, ran twice for the provincial Conservatives in North Toronto, and finally retired as a trustee in 1973. Six months later Education Minister Thomas Wells made him chairman of a panel to evaluate

---

[5] See Chapter 9.

the system of school government in Metro. An example of opposition comes from Graham Scott, former high school math teacher and computer expert, who ran for better basic skills in depressed Ward 7, then got himself censured by the teaching profession for exposing the beating of children at Brant Street School. He declined to run for re-election after the bureaucracy thwarted his efforts to disclose the reading problem at city schools; he went back to the obscurity of computer programming.

Unlike city hall, where the electorate can upset priorities by electing a reform slate, the school establishment holds such a grip on its elected board that whatever happens at the polls, the bureaucracy remains the party in power. The game is set up to keep the opposition losing, which says as much about schooling as about politics.

School trustees are thought to be the local potentates of public education, the people who are answerable when things go wrong. Their names stand on the ballot every two years. Each of the city's 11 wards elects two. They elect a chairman, and he or she occupies the second-floor suite at 155 College Street, next to the Associate Director. Until 1972, the chairman had a private automobile and chauffeur to convenience his or her visiting schools, laying cornerstones, or breaking sod. In fact, the trustees serve a ritualized function in the school system, much as a Governor General does in Parliamentary politics. The difference is that the Governor General's role is clearly established; the school trustees, on the other hand, are irritable house guests in the system they were elected to govern. Their titular status is forced upon them by an overpowering bureaucracy that allows them small compensations.

For one thing, the pay is poor. The Ministry of Education will not allow ordinary trustees to be paid more than $3,600 a year. The province in 1974 proposed to increase their allowances, but only to a mere $6,000 a year. The city

The School Bureaucracy

aldermen, by contrast, receive $15,000 a year. As parttimers, trustees cannot hope to get the grasp of the system in less than a year. The Toronto school system has an annual budget comparable to that of City Council, and it employs more people. The school board deals — not in the simple tangibles of streets, zoning bylaws, housing and sewers — but with learning theories, human behaviour, teacher-pupil ratios, and the daily welfare of 103,000 children and adolescents. The provincial government lets the trustees do this on their own time, working nights and weekends, because it wants trustees to play a token role in school affairs. The Conservative government in 1973 made this the more certain by requiring election every two years, instead of every three, ensuring a perpetual cadre of neophytes on the board.

Trustees, for their part, fall uneasily into their role. They sense the rise of citizen power beneath them, but they find themselves stymied by the bureaucracy, and disconcerted by their own lack of clarity. So they major in trivia. Should a golden trowel be given to the trustee who breaks ground for a new school? Does the director deserve a limousine? Should the word "acting" be deleted from the title of an assistant superintendent? Dare smoking be permitted in the Board Chamber? Should the meeting adjourn? These are items they have control over, things they can get safely fierce about.

Information is the grist of decision making. Any policy maker worth his ballot wants to have all pertinent information at hand. If it is not available, he will use what he can get his hands on, and that is where the bureaucracy protects its own.

Until late 1973, Toronto school trustees simply could not get the information they needed to govern. They not only couldn't get it; they proved they didn't want it. In 1972, Trustee Barnes made a motion requiring the director of education to provide whatever pertinent information about the school system a trustee might request. The Board rejected Barnes' motion by a vote of 10-8.

A year later, the trustees were still wrangling over information, still not entirely satisfied, and still not bold enough to demand more. As things stood, trustees could get information only at board or committee meetings if a majority agreed to request an official report, a request that could take two years to fulfill. Trustee Douglas Barr, a social worker who replaced Scott in Ward 7, looked back on the Barnes' vote as "one of the most serious decisions that board made."

The issue before them that February night was Director Jones' report "on a policy", the order paper said, "to differentiate between the class of information considered to be available to an individual trustee on that trustee's request and the class of information considered to be available only to all trustees by a report." This report had been requested by the board 2½ years before.

Trustee David Shanoff, lucky enough to survive the intervening election, made as polite a speech as he was able, noting that it was three years now since the battle began. "As we all know, authority and power in political decision making lies where the information is. In the past three years, some of us have felt we were reduced to rubber stamping what had already been decided by administrators. Some of us are fed up with the status of rubber stamps. Some of us would like a change."

Director Jones assured trustees that any lack of information had been a matter purely of "mechanics, logistics and shortage of staff." His staff had no wish to hold back anything. Yet his report said certain things should be withheld. Barr asked him to clarify that. Jones rose again, as

The School Bureaucracy

sincere a man as ever defended anything. He had tendered his resignation that same night, for reasons of health. What should be withheld? Personal records of students, psychological and confidential information on staff, and "trustees' expense accounts". That was all.

Cheers and applause went up from teachers in the gallery. Jones had done it again. That last phase — 'trustees' expense accounts" — was the ringer, making it seem he had secret information they wouldn't want him to tell. The ploy harkened back to the good old days, when the trustee-administrator compact thrived on complaisance. Those happy times culminated in the sad spring of 1969, when four Toronto trustees felt the need to attend the American Choral Directors and Music Educators conference in Honolulu — at Toronto taxpayers' expense. It was four days in the sun, with *Globe and Mail* reporter Ross Munro trailing their every step, and recording their every excuse for the folks back home. This episode, along with an exorbitant $74,000 farewell by North York trustees for their retiring director, upset the voting public just slightly. It was the following fall when 16 new trustees took seats on the Toronto board, including Barnes and Shanoff.

Among the first things to fall was the junket fund, (Fiona Nelson called it the Magical Mystery Tour Convention Policy) and with it fell a pillar of trustee-administrator solidarity. With trustees taking what junkets they needed (within very liberal limits), and administrators refusing to disclose the facts, even to fellow trustees (except at official board request), each side did well by the other. With a few questionable junkets under his belt, what trustee is going to complain loudly about administrative excess? A cozy relationship allowed the administrators to run the system as they knew best.

Reports are one legitimate source of information, and the trustees fell to seeking reports so ardently that the 1970 board had requested 479 within 2½ years. At one time, in August 1972, 62 reports were outstanding at one time. Report writing was done by superintendents or assistant superintendents, who are $32,000-a-year people, and anything having to do with policy had to reflect the director's views. Shanoff once said the idea of highly paid superintendents doing these reports was as sickening to him as the idea of $25,000-a-year principals going around measuring the length of girls' skirts, and Trustee William Ross added insult by saying most reports aren't worth the paper anyway. "We get the most ludicrous reports I think possible. . . . Our reports are so edited and vetted that what we get oftentimes isn't worth getting."

And so it went with report writing. The trend under Education Director Graham Gore was toward terse, cryptic reports, not to confuse the trustees with too many facts. Under Ronald Jones' regime, the Gore tactic slowly gave way to that of documentary overkill. Minor reports could still be terse and cryptic; major reports had to be long, exhaustive, replete with statistics, redolent with facts, and cryptic. The bureaucracy began to come through, as in the case of Edward McKeown's forays into special education, with great statistical data and clinical detail. It was still couched in superlatives, as in this bit of McKeownesque: "Every one of these changes was a result of a desire on the part of all concerned to meet more effectively the needs of the exceptional children who are the Board's responsibility and the continuing series of changes reflects completely the philosophy of supporting and maintaining every exceptional child in the regular program whenever possible." Now how could you refute that?

Such gleaming armour provoked a counter charge by Trustees Barr, Gordon Cressy and Dan Leckie. They set up a method of getting information that for a short time outwitted the system, and allowed at least one fine report to be written. That was the report: Vocational Schools in Toronto. With the expert help of Donald Rutledge, then director of the Language Study Centre, six trustees in two months put together a report that laid out in clear, direct prose what the vocational schools were doing, and pointed out some remedies. It was by all accounts the first time the system had the temerity to take an honest, critical look at itself.

This small coterie of like-minded trustees and a few allies later bucked the old guard to set up similar work groups on student rights, social work, and multiculturalism, each time with a modicum of success — at least in clarifying the issues. It was one glimmer of change in an otherwise obdurate arrangement.

The system's careful use of information at the top illustrates what it does at lower levels. Every bit of information is weighed for its probable impact. It is in keeping for the principal of Harbord Collegiate Institute to ban student leaflets for their criticism of teaching staff, as Ralph Haist did in 1973. Or for the principal of Forest Hill Collegiate to suspend a student for calling him in print "a paper tiger", as Hylbert Mosey did in 1969. When Professor John Eisenberg put this latter incident into a high school curriculum on current affairs, the Minister of Education refused to place that book on Circular 14, the Ministry's approved list of school textbooks. It was rejected on grounds that it contained accounts of actual people that could cause embarrassment.[6]

Private sessions are another way to control information. The private session invites abuse because the safeguards of public access to school board business are only scantily spelled out in law. Prior to 1970, the Toronto board left most of its touchy matters to the confines of private ses-

[6] "Some Books on Reality" by Bob Davis, *Community Schools,* March 1974, p.26.

sions and closed committees. In 1970 the new trustees swept in with declamations of openness. Almost all committees were made open to the press almost all the time, and items they tried to conceal usually leaked out anyway, making a mockery of what little secrecy did survive.

But by 1973, secrecy was coming back. Fiona Nelson, who as a teacher had been censured in private and before election claimed no need for private meetings, was now chairing them. Private sessions of the board, ostensibly only for issues of personnel, wages, and property purchase slowly included more and more items.

On June 14, 1973, for example, the board in private received a report from Director Jones concerning the number of students suspended during the month of May. What was on that report? In its wisdom, the board chose not to let anyone know.

That night the board also received — in private — from the Metro Toronto School Board, proposals for salary adjustments for the highest paid members of the bureaucracy. These proposals were passed in secret to the subcommittee appointed to conduct discussions with the Association of Schedule II Employees, a negotiating body for top officials. The public was not to know what "adjustments" were being made in salaries ranging from $28,000 to $39,500 until after they had been passed in private. Thus the system attempted to avoid an embarrassing public debate at a time when budget cutbacks were forcing class sizes to be increased by an average of two pupils a class in the elementary schools. At a later meeting this item did get put on the public agenda when several trustees objected to handling it in private, and the senior administrators got their raises, to a top salary of $40,500 for the director.

Another private item at that June 14 meeting was the appointment of principals for 1973-74. Trustees received a list they hadn't seen before which gave all the proposed

The School Bureaucracy

changes. A round of bitter fighting resulted. The trustees were used to rubber stamping the choices, but this time some trustees started wondering why. Cottingham Public School, for example, lost its principal to Deer Park Public School, despite protests of the community and the fuming of Trustee Fiona Nelson. "I don't know when those bureaucrats will realize it isn't just a matter of shifting a bunch of faces around," she said later.

The night of June 14 was a turning point for Trustee Cressy, Barr and Leckie, who broke briefly with the protocol of secrecy. They later managed to get some small changes in the way high school principals are chosen. But that took months of time, and while it showed some change was possible, its cost of energy and time made it more token than real.

When Duncan Green and Edward McKeown moved to positions of director and associate director of the Toronto City Board in 1973, they opened up the books. Trustees were all but surfeited in reports, done up in McKeown's statistical style. By this time, the pressures from the province and Metro had grown so strong that board and administration pulled together as a somewhat more united front with teachers in the face of the Great Avenger. But the underlying base of power shifted only slightly, and while Toronto opened out, the *Metro* Toronto School Board retained its high-handed grip on the system.

The Metro Toronto School Board, made up of trustee delegates from the city and five boroughs, began in 1953 as a noble half-way-to-amalgamation experiment in school government. It had charge mainly of finances, but as money became tighter its power grew. As nearly as I can see it today, it serves three main purposes: (1) it provides an economic and political buffer between city and province, (2) it places on neighboring school divisions the onus of achieving equity among themselves, and (3) it strengthens the hold of the bureaucracy, and hence the province, on school government.

Metro Toronto School Board meetings are noteworthy for their lack of passion, and the reason for the happy accord lies largely in the fact that most of the business is done behind the scenes. At the Metro level, like nowhere else, the technocrats handle school business.

Administrators of all the area boards are tied together in an immense web of interlocking committees. In 1972, for example, there were 10 sub-committeees with "ongoing" responsibilities, including such things as planning, psychological services, finance, group life insurance, and communications. There were also 12 sub-committees with "periodic" responsibilities, six sub-committees on budget, six study committees and two staff-allocation committees.

All of these were filled with administrators or teachers. No elected trustees sat on any of them. They did not report to the Metro Toronto School Board, but to an elite body of administrators called the Advisory Council of Directors. This is made up of the directors of each board, salaries ranging from $42,000 to $45,000, who meet weekly in private, usually on Wednesday morning.

This group deliberates the pros and cons of major policy decisions, then submits its proposals to the Metro Toronto School Board. The matter then becomes public, the trustees have their turn. But of course, they debate without the benefit of knowing what went before, and without information that may be contrary to the proposal made by the Advisory Council of Directors.

This group, proposed by William McCordic in 1966 as a "Metro education cabinet" carries on completely out of the public eye and has no direct tie to the electorate. When I asked Metro board chairman Bruce Bone for permission to report on Advisory Council meetings, he refused. "This group," he said, "is clearly not a policy-making body." Then he told me what it is: "It is, in fact, the fulcrum of a

THE SCHOOL BUREAUCRACY 177

network of metro-wide staff committees maintaining a continuous assessment of items of Metro significance." Not anything the public would be interested in knowing about, to be sure.

The slogans, the grand generalities, they are the realm of the politicians, the public. It is left to the technicians to decide what the slogans mean, to interpret them in terms of the political structures they have espoused as workable. As the SEF people — technocrats par excellence — put it in their first document, it is up to the technicians, the managers, the administrators, to take those aims and goals and "clothe them with significance."[7]

The technicians, secure from political surveillance, run the system by formulae and statistical analysis that often militate against the goals they are meant to serve.

Since general statements in themselves are held to be meaningless, the technocrat is free to create meaning after the image of the technocratic auspices in which he breathes and moves, and the system of corporate enterprise that makes it all possible.[8] The establishment of the SEF schools seems to be one fine example of this phenomenon at work.

Having thus defined the situation, they have insulated themselves from political control. Trustees, as well as managers, honor the split. It is sanctified by the doctrine of separate functions: the trustees set policy, the administrators enact it.[9] But in actual fact, the flow of power is re-

---

[7] See the first chapter of *E-1: Specifications and User Requirements for Elementary Schools,* Metro Toronto School Board, 1969. For SEF, see next chapter.

[8] See George Martell's analysis of the schools within the corporate capitalist system in his introduction to *The Politics of the Canadian Public School,* James, Lewis and Samuel, 1974.

[9] Toronto trustees used the doctrine of separate functions as a club to keep one another in line. "The role of the trustee is to set general policy for the administrator to execute," Herbert Barnes declared in a public

versed. Power emanates from the centralized political mandate through bureaucracy; the function of the trustees is to legitimate it. They become a buffer between local community and educational machine.

The supposedly exalted position of political decision making becomes a debased one of talking nonsense, and the once humble role of the civil servant becomes an elite preserve of those who create options. The power is no longer with the local democratic body; it has slipped to a highly centralized command. Thus the techno-bureaucratic mold encapsulates the humanistic aims and goals of education.

On the face of it, this appears to be a very natural way for things to happen. Middle-level politicians in fact do not know what they mean by many of their own political statements. And technocrats in fact are forced to find their own way of deciding what they ought to mean. Since both sides accept the separation of policy making from administration, the two sides can co-exist. There is little interchange, no creativity, except the spawning of techniques for better education delivery. The system becomes accountable, then, to emulate the dead forms of institutional life, and to offer students a lesson in corporate schizophrenia.

Increasingly, the establishment relies on opinion polls, and hastily uses them. A survey early in 1974 showed a desire for Chinese by 316 high school students, so the educators proposed offering both Mandarin and Cantonese at Harbord Collegiate and North Toronto Collegiate at night school and summer school. It was more than the community groups had even requested.

>letter chiding Fiona Nelson for trying to set specific priorities in trimming the 1972 budget. "Too often in the last two years a small group of well-intentioned but naive trustees have erred in trying to act as directors of education." The doctrine has a certain common-sense basis, but its use in the school system is to create a shield for administrators against the intrusion of trustees, and to provide trustees with an arena they can call their own.

And the Ministry of Education itself commissioned the biggest poll ever in 1971 to find out what parents think of public schooling. Wells was happy to report to the Ontario Federation of Home and School Associations in 1972 that "85 per cent described themselves as 'moderately' to 'very' happy with the quality of education provided, and 70 per cent said that education has improved in the past five years." These mechanisms have to fill in for the lack of political interaction and ferment in the governing structures of education. The results are formalistic solutions devoid of the uniqueness and excitement that could arise out of political give and take.

The two sides stand at odds. The result is sterility of a most senseless sort. On one side stands the humanist wanting to adapt the institution to human needs, seeking a remedy for wrongs and a just distribution of the benefits of education. On the other side stand the technicians, those skilled in the technologies of organization, efficiency, cybernetics, and learning, the people who can do it. Both sides take positions within the larger logic of the bureaucratic system and the political economy that created and sustains it. Not always are these forces represented by trustee and technocrat: it is not that simple. Yet at the Board of Education the humanist impulse tends to be that tiny, ragged, frightened minority in both board and bureaucracy, posed against the imposing strength of the system pushers.

The two sides have trouble talking. The radical humanists, torn from community, clutch a fantasized ideal, and they compromise out of fear or harden out of arrogance. The technocrats are servants primarily of the mystique of efficiency and pragmatism, and secondarily of distant centralized power.

Chapter 9

THE COMING OF SEF

They all looked alike. They had walls of blank concrete slabs, windows set vertically in bunker-like façades, silhouettes that were monotonous boxes. The community people called them jails. But they were schools. And inside they had all the creature comforts. Moveable walls, padded floors, plastic furniture, open space by the acre. The places were acoustically absorbent, air-conditioned, stain-resistant and humidity controlled.

"When you have a school like this," one 12-year-old said, "you don't need to ask for anything."

He was describing how it felt inside the new SEF prototype school house, a facility built to all the latest innovations in schooling and technology. The acronym stands for Studies in Educational Facilities. It was, in fact, a $40,000,000 crash course in technical innovation, bringing to fulfillment the then Education Minister William Davis' intention "to plan the shape of future schools to avoid obsolescence, and to control costs."

SEF began in 1966. It had three main objectives. First, it would try to predict what kind of school houses would be needed in the future. Second, it would create a way of building schools on an assembly-line basis, having them fit together on the site from prefabricated components. And

The Coming of SEF

third, it would reduce school building costs. The study was supposed to last three years; it eventually lasted nine.

The fact that all 25 schools in the first SEF project bore an unmistakable resemblance was seen as an irrelevant side effect of the new functionalism. In fact, they were functionalism's finest hour in school construction, meeting as they did the diverse requirements of both schooling and technocracy.

A glance at history shows that cookie-cutter school houses are nothing new in Toronto. Indeed, the very first half-dozen common schools ever built by the Toronto Board of Education all looked alike. They featured all the newest equipment, too. They were "handsome, spacious and commodious, suitably fitted up and supplied with all needful appliances" the Board's report boasted. They included two hot-air furnaces for each school. And those first six buildings also fitted the stately architecture of that day, having neatly arched windows, stout three-story entry towers, and tiny turrets.

But let history be history.

SEF's claim to newness was its formidable assembly line-up, and its ingenious commitment to total adaptability. Not surprisingly, its impetus came in the first instance from a Ford Foundation subsidiary, a school design agency calling itself Educational Facilities Laboratory. EFL had just completed a project of four school buildings in California, and needed a place to upgrade the basic systems design. It offered schools in Metro Toronto that would be 80 per cent pre-fabricated. This northern locale held the challenge of a cold climate, the need for triple-story schools in downtown Toronto, and the amenity of a large, centralized school government.

Davis invited EFL to Ontario. He hired Architect Frank Nicol to introduce the sale, and Metro Toronto School

Board bought the SEF package without objections, with the promise of $50,000 a year from the province and the prospect of roughly $500,000 from EFL.

SEF was no mere study. It was an action program. On one hand it drew up the academic and technical requirements. It published them in six thick, glossy volumes, replete with two-color spreads and full-page photographs. On the other hand, it sold these specifications to a wary building industry, promising a ready market of one million square feet. It tendered for bids, accepted contracts, and then saw to it that all the pieces fell in place roughly on schedule. This took a prodigious display of technocratic skill, and a magnificent outlay of cash.

Luckily, SEF appeared in 1966, when the Metro educational budget was increasing by 27 per cent a year, the postwar baby boom was forcing Ontario to complete almost a school a day, and a rash of technical innovations were making the old cubicle classrooms seem untenable. The new SEF technology promised a great leap forward. This method of systems building, a way of piecing together schools like Meccano sets, had never been attempted to this extent anywhere in North America. It was a chance for Toronto to show the world what the new technology could achieve.

The objective was a school house that could adapt itself to any new educational requirement. It was to create a school environment where the progressive teacher would not be held back in any way by architecture, and to provide this adaptability at great savings in cost.

It didn't work out quite that way. The first 25 schools, including the studies that backed them up, rang up a price tag of $32.8 million, which was $4.4 million more than so many schools would have cost under the ordinary Metro cost ceiling. The SEF technicians had garnered contracts with the aid of a liberal cost-of-living escalation clause, which gave the builders an eventual bonanza — as in the case of Howard Public School — of $24.74 a square foot ($2.14 above target). Local school officials got into the act by demanding all the extras money could buy, and this too pushed up the price and expanded the market. While SEF was monopolizing Metro's school building market, other independent builders cut their profits to the bone to pick up what work they could. Ordinary school prices fell, leaving trustees to cast about with unhappy comparisons. And despite the high-powered management skills of technical director Roderick Robbie, those first SEF projects ran into constant crossfire from local officials.[1]

But out of it all came a grand total of 32 schools, with the latter six redeeming SEF by coming in under the ceiling cost of $19.50 a square foot. Anyway, $4.4 million under the bridge is small potatoes in the pyrotechnics of systems building, and the way Architect Roderick Robbie went about it, the future was sure to be indebted. He wowed the building industry with talk about systems construction putting Canada over the top. "The building industry is the sleeping giant of North America," he said by way of *The Globe and Mail*'s Report on Business. "It is going the same route as cars and aircraft. The General Motors of the building industry could be a great Canadian corporation owned 40 per cent by the federal Government, 30 per cent by Canadian companies and 30 per cent by individual Cana-

---

[1] Architect Howard Walker headed up an ad hoc committee of the Ontario Association of Architects that reported on SEF in October 1971: "Throughout the initial stages to completion, considerable confusion existed due to the chain of command with sub-system contractors who were selected by Metro but hired by the area boards under a project manager also hired by the area boards. In addition, SEF standards set by Metro conflicted with the boards' standards. The architects were faced with a multiplicity of directives from all sides with no clearcut definition of who was responsible for what."

dian investors." He also impressed the educators by telling them they were being held back by their schools. "Present school architecture is hooked on regimented space," he told *Globe and Mail* reporter Barrie Zwicker. "The new approach to education, which accepts the process of unpredictable change, requires the flowering of a new dynamic architecture of speculative space."

These words put iron in the blood. SEF set out on its first building project in great spirits, with hardly a word about it in the press, and only a hazy notion among school trustees as to what they were getting into. It seemed good enough to them that the Ministry backed it up, and that the technocrats would make it work.

At the upper end of an asphalt play field stands Roden Public School, an SEF school. It is one of the first five, a model for the entire system. Sombre concrete walls three stories high, narrow windows looking out at motley-colored gables of surrounding homes. Each concrete slab measures 10 feet by 10; they fit together like building blocks, and the whole effect is that of a fortress. This is the school the neighbors called "the jail" at first, until principal Donald Irwin disabused them of it. "We were the guinea pigs," Irwin told me. "This was the prototype for the system." He had been getting over 1,000 visitors a year, mainly from Boston and Chicago. The school had 1,024 children, 53 teachers, and had been operating 2½ years. Patently, it was working, and the scenes inside were common to open schooling anywhere.

In one Grade 1 class, three boys played with Lego, two others made a tunnel of cardboard blocks, two pieced together plastic puzzles, and one boy drew pictures. Five girls were painting at another table. Two boys worked at the sandbox, while eight children practiced reading with the teacher at a round table in the far corner. A boy scurried from sandbox to teacher's lap. The lesson continued.

Another boy sat idly alone at a large table picking his fingernails. The place was colorful to distraction. Long paper streamers hung from the ceiling making little nooks. Every corner seemed full of cut-outs, mobiles and models.

At another teaching station, another regimen. A teacher dressed tidily in blue struck a gong. The children froze in position and raised their hands above their heads. "You two are making too much noise," she shouted, "and I'm not going to talk to you about it again. Now put your hands down and get to work." A moment later she grabbed an unruly boy by the shoulder. "What's the matter?" she scolded, "you've been being really good up to now." Another child escaped into the open space and she rushed after.

The teacher could not contend with free space; she unwittingly transformed it into another kind of jail. Irwin told me this place had a way of bringing out the immaturities. "If you are going to exist in this sort of place, you've got to mature pretty quickly or you're not going to make it." This was why Irwin deliberately worked on human relationships the first years, helping teachers to learn the art of cooperation. Six class areas opened onto a common activity area, and sheer numbers forced the teachers to be constantly on the alert. It used to be four solid walls that held the children in. Now it was the teacher's voice and training. But if it allowed room for mishap, it also allowed room for growth. There was a chance of mutual support, here, too, if teachers could rise to it.

It can be a school, it can be a barn. People can always redeem the facilities or flout them. But Irwin found the school spoke a positive message, and when I asked him what he meant he said: "If one of our aims is to develop versatile human beings, this is an environment that permits it." He admitted that any school space could be used well, that Adam Beck, a traditional school, is "ahead of us in a lot of ways. You can do it in a tent, if you have to, I suppose," he said. "But these features improve our chances, and it's yet to be seen if we will make use of them."

At other schools, it became clear that openness had other uses, too. Even at Roden, Irwin spoke of the "domino effect," by which new teaching strategies and classroom decor swept the school. One teacher would start hanging streamers from the ceiling to create more secluded nooks and crannies, and soon other teachers were doing it. "Things travel at a rather rapid rate at a place like this."

The open classrooms, though not legalistically imposed, were in tune with the neo-progressive ethos that swept most teachers into new arrangements. It put the entire school much more at the principal's fingertips, and created a watchful consensus, a tendency toward self-governing uniformity. A class or teacher that got too loud caused a general disturbance, and the sounds of an engrossing lesson next door made some teachers appreciate the old-fashioned luxury of walls.

But all in all, the euphoria of putting a new machine through its paces, and the extreme attention paid to this extravaganza to make it work, result in relatively happy arrangements. SEF schools were prizes; the best principals went there. And they were richly endowed with teaching devices. At Roden these included ten TV sets, six film projectors, 23 tape recorders, 20 tape players at the start. Each space was supplied with furniture of all sizes, specially designed for SEF but sometimes hard to get repaired. When a teacher complained to Irwin that she needed a book shelf, he suggested the most convenient thing would be for her to bring in some bricks and boards.

A breakdown at a SEF school entailed calling a specialist. A mere stationary engineer could not service the atmosphere control. He would need a 10-week course. Canada Electric Co., Ltd., a service agency for J.W. Swanson & Associates of Buffalo, which gets its heating-air conditioning units from the Nesbitt Division of the International Telephone and Telegraph (ITT) Company in Philadelphia, supplied these components. The company was a little put out that SEF did not enter into a five-year service contract as well. Such were the complications of the new technology.

SEF was an open building system — the first, Robbie said, in history — whereby the school building would be broken into 10 basic parts to be fitted together like a block puzzle on site.

The parts, called subsystems or components, included structure, atmosphere, lighting-ceiling, vertical skin, plumbing, electric-electronic, caseworks and furniture, roofing, and interior finish. A company would bid on one component, and the lowest bidder got to supply that component to all the 25 schools. The SEF management team saw to it that all the subsystems fit together on site. "A building system," as Robbie explained it, "was a set of building parts which had been conceived and manufactured to assemble without adjustment or waste." For example, it wouldn't do for a plumber to have to bore holes in walls to install his pipes. The holes had to be anticipated.

Robbie had guided the system until 1969, when he ended his $20,000-a-year SEF stint to return to private architecture and town planning, leaving subordinates to finish the job. Meanwhile, the academic side of things was under the charge of Hugh Vallery, former principal of Monarch Park Secondary School, an easily adaptive counterpart. Vallery led the teams of academic advisors and writers who turned out the books of user requirements. These books came out about the same time as the technical studies did.

By its own criteria, SEF succeeded in every way except in saving money. It was a touchy point, considering the fact that Robbie predicted in 1968 that the schools would be 30 per cent more useful while costing 10 per cent less. Trustees who wakened to the magnitude of SEF in 1972 fastened on cost as the big item. SEF nearly lapsed in 1972 when Bruce Bone in his inaugural as Metro School Board Chairman, hinted that SEF might have to be put on the shelf, and William McCordic, Metro board director, commented that SEF may have come five years too late "for us to continue the process and take advantage of the savings."

Bruce Bone looked ruefully at Denlow Avenue Public School, a gray elephant two blocks from his North York home. At $24 a square foot, quite an expensive monument to functionalism. Ernest Avenue Public School across town was built for $16 a square foot — outside of SEF. And in downtown Toronto, Kensington Community School went up tailored by the local residents for a square foot cost of only $16.40.

The issues trustees grasped were cost and efficiency, and on this point the technicians finally convinced them to keep trying. Stage 2 began as something of a rescue effort. To have stopped after having offered so much, with money the only bugaboo, would have cast the entire operation in a shadow. Gerald Phillips, a young Scarborough trustee who had been made chairman of SEF Advisory Committee, admitted that the first 25 had cost too much, that the economical gains "can't be proved at this point", and that the utility of SEF schools was neither inferior nor superior by all objective tests. "We must have faith," he told me, "that the SEF approach is logical."[2]

Yet if they cost more, a case could be made that they were worth more. SEF's carpets would not cause hay

[2] SEF's utility to the building industry of North America was quite apparent in the reasons put before the Metro School Board in 1970 urging an extension: "Discontinuation of the SEF Building System would have a very detrimental effect on the progress of systems building development, not only in Ontario and Canada, but indeed for the entire North American continent, because of the impact of SEF system on the North American building scene." From the Metro Toronto School Board Minutes, Dec. 8, 1970, p. 605.

fever, its atmosphere control minimized colds, its lighting was less bright and better for the eyes, its acoustics were soft, its heating system maximized fuel usage. The lighting system cost more than normal to install, but it used half the number of fluorescent tubes. The gymnasium — Tartan floors, acoustical ceilings and atmosphere control — cost $4 a square foot more than ordinary gyms with unsprung hardwood floors, exposed joists and no air conditioning. Peter Tirion, SEF's latter-day technical director, pointed out that there was far more use in an SEF gym. SEF's quality control testing, said Tirion, was "probably 10 times higher than in traditional construction."

But others had plenty of complaints. John Hackett, project architect at Arlington, was having a bad day when my colleague Peter Mosher visited the school for a series we were writing about SEF. Water stood an inch deep in the "cafetorium" and a large section of carpeted corridor. Six caretakers worked four hours to clean it all up. Hackett commented: "Everything in the system seems to disregard the fact that kids will be using it. Nothing's quite heavy enough. Perhaps it's a cost factor. Contractors lower quality of products to the bone to bid low and get the contract." Mosher reported later that "new buildings have bugs, and it seems that complex new buildings have complex bugs." He found that bookcases had collapsed, a movie screen above a blackboard and a basketball net in the gym had fallen, the air conditioning alternated between too hot and too cold, public address speakers didn't work, clocks jumped ahead and bells rang at strange intervals. For all that, Arlington Principal John Condie said it was still better than previous buildings he taught in, despite the fact that it was more flexible than the builders had intended.

Our inquiry threw doubt on SEF's technical prowess, though some of its improvements would doubltess prove themselves in time. A study done by an independent research team, David Jackson and Associates, showed teachers and pupils as pleased with their SEF schools as with any others but not more so.

For all that expense it embarrassed SEF people a trifle that they failed to please absolutely, though the failure could always be laid to the people not knowing how to use their new facilities. One young architectural student, Grant Wanzel, probably put the case most succinctly: "The structural system within the stated objectives is an improvement over existing schools, although in fact none of this has anything to do with how people learn."

The argument based on cost was one that fit the narrow political scope of school trustees. It was clearly an easy target for critics. But SEF's basic intent did not get carefully scrutinized in the political arena, either at the start or later on. The issue seemed too large and complicated, it was too well taken care of by the technocrats. Bruce Bone was to lament years later that he didn't think they knew at the time what they were getting into. "When the idea of SEF was put forward, I wasn't aware it was going to evolve as it did, and I'm not sure many trustees did."

SEF's lack was not its failure to measure up, but in its failure to begin at the beginning. The designers of SEF said at the outset they could not revamp the entire educational system, they would have to work within its given structures. Having said that, they delved into social and educational theory to find a foundation for what they intended to build. The inquiry resulted in the discovery that children and teachers should be doing what this new technology was ready to make possible.

What becomes fairly clear from a review of the three books setting out the user requirements was that SEF philosophy was the school system's own mixture of behaviorism and progressivism, with a strong dash of technocratic bravura. Its analysis starts out with an appropriately scary tone, inducing a hyped liberal awareness that makes technological cures so sweet. "The social fabric of the family, the city, the nation, indeed the whole world seems to be shivering and about to grind itself apart," says a sentence in *Patterns for Change*. Indeed, all this, SEF comforts us, may be only "the birth pangs of a golden age." And how is that? We are given many home truths as the SEF periscope scans the horizon. One fine illustration of the technological mind-set is its reference to contraceptive devices.

Many people today, SEF says, "were not deliberately conceived, they happened rather by accident as a result of their parents' behavior." Given this sad state of affairs, people are likely to doubt their own value. But for this trouble, too, technology has an answer. "Hopefully, in the coming decades, when practically all children will be deliberately conceived, every human will be more secure in his feelings about his own value and self-worth." SEF's penchant for prediction and control continues in another selection: "Only by the deliberate creation of long-range and predictive educational planning systems can problems of learning, teaching, curriculum, educational finance and school building design be resolved." It just happens to be the case that many matters in education are not open to prediction and control; to assume that they are affects the spontaneity of learning. Perhaps realizing this, SEF turns a corner to say, in its first book: "The only unqualified prediction we are prepared to make is that in the foreseeable future there will be greater overall variability."

If it foresaw a wide open future, SEF favored behaviorism for the present. "To teach someone is, first of all, to form a clear intention to modify his beliefs — and, consequently, his behavior," says the first SEF book. But SEF was also influenced by progressive thought. It mentioned the humanist critics approvingly, and tried for a blend of behaviorism with the accoutrements of progressivism. But finally, SEF philosophy came down to pragmatism. Here its commitment was to be clear and unyielding:

> The ultimate criterion against which this Report must be judged is its utility. To what extent does the Report help educators and designers to develop more functional school accommodations? This test can be made only as persons responsible for planning new facilities try to use it.[3]

Alas, the internal structures of SEF itself seemed to deny this. A host of advisory committees were set up to oversee the work, but simply by default they represented chiefly bureaucrats and technicians. For example, the group on intermediate school classrooms included three principals, one school inspector, one principal-designate, three superintendents and no teachers. The teachers were too busy teaching. The SEF Advisory Committee itself included five administrators, five trustees, four engineers, and three architects. No parents, teachers, or students. Few of the communities into which the SEF schools were placed had any say about them in advance.

The study by David Jackson & Associates found that parents visited traditional schools informally more often than they did SEF or other open schools. The consultants' general conclusion was this: "From the standpoint of the users, all things considered, the new open plan non-SEF schools were just as satisfactory as SEF schools."

To SEF's devotees, the concept of total flexibility inspired a heady iconoclasm in the planning offices. But in fact the schools were not totally flexible. The concrete outer walls stood, no matter what — they couldn't even be

---

[3] *SEF El: Educational Specifications and User Requirements for Elementary (K-6) Schools*, Metro Toronto School Board, 1968.

defaced — and the inner walls weren't collapsible at the push of a button. The 1971 report by the Ontario Association of Architects pointed out, for example, that SEF still hadn't shown the steel relocatable walls to be any easier to move than an ordinary drywall or concrete block partition.[4] It took a weekend to move a wall, and most school principals just didn't bother, causing Architect John Hackett to wonder: "If things don't get moved, is the school really more flexible?"

But the possibilities boggled the minds. The SEF people devoted themselves so joyously to the technocratic dream that they saw their creation as an ideological abstraction. "Let the building get out of the way of education and give us total flexibility" was one SEF slogan, and John Murray spoke about the SEF structures almost as if they were anti-matter. "We changed the emphasis dramatically in the architecture of the school. We've changed it from a pretty thing, from a monument, to a building that has functional use in the community. We de-emphasized style and re-emphasized function."

It was true within limits. The new structures could not be accused of looking pretty, but it was hardly true that their functional conversion made them into mute servants to the local educational whim. Quite the opposite. The schools were still monuments. But monuments to what? The overall message — if these buildings had a message at all — seemed to be the one identified with Western civilization by George Grant — "that the pursuit of technological efficiency is the chief purpose for which the community exists." And their harsh packaging stamped the whole endeavor with the imprint of centralized control. SEF re-emphasized function within the verities of a technocratic order. Schooling was not yet to be a creation of the local

---

[4] See page 5 of the October 1971 report, "An Evaluation of the SEF Building Program."

community, but a tribute to the technocracy that put it there. One quiet contrast to this new mode was Kensington Community School, built over the same period according to plans mulled over and approved by local residents, a unique, red brick design with large shake gables. It is a monument, too — to school-community cooperation.

SEF suited the overall trend of the 1960's toward centralized control on the one hand, and neo-progressive schooling on the other. As symbols of the new regimen, SEF's outside shell made a rather abrasive intrusion into local communities, while its interiors were opened up to the neo-progressive practices of team teaching and free movement. The shell was hard and obdurate, the internal structure wieldy and adaptable.

The SEF booklets, meanwhile, projected educational needs to suit the technological possibilities. They went so far as to speculate that someday lights may dim and brighten automatically at school to simulate clouds moving across the sun. "The changes might be restful to the eye." Flexibility was a commodity technology was ready to deliver; SEF enlisted it for education and for the building industry that stood ready to provide it.

The SEF visionaries had not been able, by the very parameters of their study, to push their functionalism one step further — into the essence of community itself. SEF found its inspiration for functionalism within the bureaucracy of schooling. What it could not take seriously — though Robbie mentioned it as an eventual possibility — was the prospect of a decentralized school, in which students would utilize existing facilities in the community and be organized loosely in learning groups, without having any one building as schoolhouse.

Another pertinent community matter was the size of the new schools. On this important point, the technocrats use educational theory and economics to rationalize enormity. The local residents were not asked. A capacity of 825 primary pupils seemed best, even though almost nobody who used them liked schools that big. Principal Irwin told me straight out about Roden: "This school's too big — it should be half this size." But the technocrats carried the day with the plausible argument that schools with fewer than 550 pupils "might not adequately support educational practices such as non-grading and co-operative teaching which are designed to individualize learning opportunities." It was all so very well put. Of course, they added as an afterthought, there were economic factors, too. Small schools just couldn't justify all the "ancillary and service area allotments" of a large school.

SEF did not trouble itself with the hiatus between school and community. This had been the unenviable topic of a side study commissioned to Grant Wanzel, a graduate of the University of Toronto School of Architecture, who worked for six months to write a research report for SEF called "The Place of the School in the Community." This report was never distributed by SEF; the SEF Advisory Committee decided against it. Murray said it wasn't technically good enough. Wanzel said the SEF leadership simply couldn't stomach his findings. At any rate, Wanzel's report was a polite rebuke to the assumptions underlying SEF.

He said appropriate facilities couldn't be planned at all without local community involvement. As it was, local residents were often hostile but always interested, educators were often rejecting and somewhat self-satisfied. "Therefore," said Wanzel, "they are not likely to seek more contact, or change the present structure." He also declared that local involvement in both facility planning and child-centred learning was absolutely essential. "As the present hierarchic and centralized education system appears to inhibit contact and involvement at the local level, it is suggested that efforts be made to decentralize...."

This was hardly the stuff SEF was made of. Wanzel's report swiftly slid into limbo. He quit SEF angry over official attempts to water down his conclusions, and later joined an educational community called Counterfoil, oriented around the ideas of Ivan Illich. I visited him one day on the second floor of an old semi-detached house on Major Street. "See, this house is a good example of flexibility," he told me. "It's been lived in by many different kinds of people, and used in many different ways. The house can be adapted. It is as flexible as people make it. Nothing is prescribed. But the initiative has to come from the people living here. SEF anticipates all the moves, it anticipates the future. And it says the future will happen on a five-foot grid."

Chapter 10

THE DAVIS IMPERATIVE

The scene is the swank Skyline Hotel, an architectural sprawl at the northwest corner of Metro Toronto. It stands in one of those tattered ecological wastelands that spring up like brambles around major airports. A massive hydroelectric transit station out back, a noisy clutter of expressways out front, DC-10's and Boeing 747's rumbling along the air approach overhead, and nothing but ornate luxury inside. The Skyline was the place for the seventh annual conference of the Ontario School Trustees' Council and the Ontario Institute for Studies in Education. The theme was the politics of education. It drew a prim horde of clean-cut, suited and tied, dedicated educationists from the entire province at $25.00 a head.

Harry Fisher, a big, suave man, reminds his audience that in Canada, education is first and foremost a provincial matter. He quotes the British North America Act as evidence. He is director of supervisory services for the Ministry of Education, ever on the alert for alien influences, always concerned with purity of purpose. It irks him that discussion groups, as he put it, "are being imbedded by American researchers." This is a dig at the likes of Laurence Iannaccone, a professor formerly of OISE, who flew in from the University of California at Riverside to give a major speech.

Fisher defines the Canadian reality by describing school boards as "sub-organizations". They might as well know they exist by the grace of the provincial Government, the goose that lays golden eggs. Later, Iannaccone called it nonsense: "No senior government delegates this structural base of local power out of the goodness of its heart," he told the delegates. "Political demand based on moral conviction of people better explains the thrust for school district sovereignty."

But Fisher had present-day reality in mind. "In a very real sense, the Ministry formulates the philosophy within which educational opportunities will be offered, calls upon local authorities to fill in the detail of the pattern, and then offers assistance in a variety of forms to those authorities in a common endeavor to achieve effective results."

No qualms about self-determination here. School boards, Fisher said, "while they effect postures of sovereignty . . . can never be sovereign. What these posturings do accomplish, however, is a constant adjustment in the legal umbilical which acts as the constitutional bond between the Ministry and the school boards. Some would call this adjustment the process of maturing decentralization."

Others would call it plain old paternalism. But not Louis McGill, director of the Grey County Board of Education, who sat on the panel as if to be the spokesman for local autonomy. Being devil's advocate was plainly not his bag of tea. "We are not working against one another," he assured everyone, "but for one another," and he ended his speech with a salutory quotation from Education Minister Thomas Wells. It was his conviction that the province would give school boards more power as they came to deserve it. "Controls will be reduced in direct proportion to the degree to which boards will be able to function in their own roles." It was only too clear that McGill, along with all 150 directors of education in Ontario, held his power by the grace of the Ministry of Education.

Toronto trustee Fiona Nelson, dressed in floppy black hat, and black suit, sitting in the fifth row, quickly spotted McGill's allegiance. "That's similar to saying when you demonstrate that you're going to vote our way we'll give you the vote," she exclaimed. "To my mind, that's the worst form of Uncle Tomism."

Toronto trustee Mary Fraser, sitting beside her — floppy green hat, blue-and-white striped suit — asked McGill when he thinks the Ministry is going to "set the boards free." He allowed that the Ministry probably really should appreciate local expectations more clearly.

"But in three years have they done it?" she asked.

"No, they haven't," McGill replied.

Fisher didn't see the problem. "I made a count in 1969 of the decision points that the boards of education have," he said. "There are 269 individual decision points. And I think in the next few years there will be more. I don't understand what you mean by 'setting the boards free.' I think we are blessed — or cursed, depending on your point of view — with an unretractable umbilical."

This irritated Trustee Fraser. "We do the dirty work while they make the decisions," she fumed.

And from the back row, Lincoln County board director G. Roger Allen: "It is called in this province centralized control and decentralized blame." That definition later entered the jargon in the upper reaches of educational government as an "Allenism."

People who wanted free public education back in 1780 also faced resistance at the top. Governor John Simcoe who had fought against republicanism in the South, didn't want it spreading in Upper Canada. Schooling for the ruling class promised some security, and Simcoe called John Strachan from Scotland to set up, not a common school, but a university. This design failed. Strachan eventually took over the first Grammar School at York. It was no university, but it was exclusive, and it was Anglican. It was also government-financed, but the poor could not attend.

A popularly elected Legislature managed to pass the Common School Act in 1816. This was the first centralized effort toward public schooling in Ontario. It provided a modest grant toward setting up schools wherever 20 pupils could be found. Until that time, says Historian William Fleming, the Legislature had proved itself indifferent — or downright hostile — to popular education. The real power in Upper Canada was the Executive Council controlled by the Family Compact which took an even dimmer view of popular education.

The townspeople of York started a two-storey school in the south-east corner of College Square and hired a headmaster, but as an attempt at democratic schooling it was too early. It failed. Within four years the Family Compact closed it down by simply cutting off the grant. Jesse Ketchum and his two fellow trustees had to resign; the teacher was fired. Then John Strachan, a right-hand man of God and the Family Compact, who now headed up the District Board, reopened the school under a new name and new patronage. Three government officials were appointed to run it. The school was back in the lap of the Family Compact. A parental boycott faded, and 10 years later 338 children were getting the three R's with grammar, bookkeeping and geography, and strong doses of Anglicanism. All but 10 of the very poorest, selected by lot, had to pay. Free education was yet to come.

Jesse Ketchum (this city's first industrialist; he owned a tannery; they called him Uncle Jesse), not to be stopped, went into legislative politics, where he joined that other maverick, William Lyon Mackenzie, to represent York in the Upper Canada Legislature. Another friend of Ketchum's was Egerton Ryerson. Both were Methodists. When Ketchum was vice-president of the York Temperance Society, Ryerson was secretary.

They had a common foe in John Strachan, but Strachan had his considerable virtues. In 1813, for example, he had urged U.S. Commodore Isaac Chauncey to hold back his plundering troops, after the retreating British general set a fuse to 500 barrels of gunpowder and blew up 200 Americans. Strachan's entreaties saved most of the town, but the U.S. soldiers did burn down the Parliament buildings. Two years later the British burned Washington in return. When ex-President Thomas Jefferson complained about this "brutality," John Strachan put a question to him in an open letter: "Can you tell me, sir, the reason why the public buildings and library of Washington should be held more sacred than those at York?"[1] So Strachan had respect as well as power. He was Harry Fisher's true predecessor, striving to protect the local entity from American domination on one hand, while taking it under centralized control with the other. The theme is recurrent in Ontario educational history.

Consolidation was one of Ryerson's constantly thwarted latter-day ambitions. He repeatedly tried to bring the schools into larger governmental units, to meet the needs of the new industrial state. But the people were not with him on this, as they had been on free education and property taxation. Even though the School Act of 1850 permitted townships to set up consolidated boards, only one had done so 21 years later. During the 1860's Ryerson repeatedly urged the county school conventions to support his plans to make school mergers easier, all for nothing. He drew up a whole series of bills to provide for township boards, but the Legislature always turned them down. This resistance lasted right into the 1920's, when Education Minister G.H. Ferguson tried to put through a bill to set up township school boards. Historian William Fleming writes the epitaph to that effort:

[1] Which may account for the fact that Toronto alderman William Kilbourn, an historian, honored Strachan as "the real founder of Ontario" in the *Toronto Citizen,* Dec. 1973.

"Trustees in the existing boards put up such strong resistance . . . that the bill . . . was withdrawn." And so long after Ryerson's time, the central government pushed for larger units, but always — until recent years — against strong and successful opposition.

During the 1930's, it became a game among inspectors to see how many boards could be persuaded to amalgamate. In 1930 was when the province appointed all public school inspectors centrally, rather than let county councils or the school boards themselves choose them. Yet Fleming reports curiously that while school districts got larger and school trustees more prestigious, it didn't really improve the efficiency of schooling.

But the province persisted, and what finally broke the back of local resistance was legislation in 1964 that decreed each township would henceforth be a school district. This broke the 150-year-old tradition of local determination of district boundaries. It reduced the number of elementary boards from 2,236 to 889. But also, as David Cameron notes, it undercut the basis of local resistance to what would come later.

In 1969, the province took the last big step; it established 76 county-sized school districts, and the entire scale of public education was transformed.

Davis' two salesmen of amalgamation, Thomas Houghton and George Waldrum, described the 1964 move as fulfilling what Ryerson had tried to achieve 100 years before. As they saw it, education would finally have a rational, technically feasible, organizational base. But they failed to see that during those 100 years since Ryerson first attempted it, the earth had shifted under their feet.

Houghton, who later sprang from the Ministry to the directorship of York Board of Education, showed a fatherly tolerance of those who cried foul. "This resistance to change is a thing that will change only in time," he said in an interview in 1970, "as parents get the feeling that this is better for their children." It was, in any case; the fruit of concentrated effort. Waldrum, who moved up to Deputy Minister when Ed Stewart followed Davis to the premier's office, made like Churchill with the words: "We had a background here of 25 years of sweat and toil upon which this thing was built. That's why it worked. Other places it went bang. They didn't have 25 years of sweat and toil."

Probably only in a parliamentary system could a change this drastic have been carried out so fast.[2] For all that, Davis laid his groundwork carefully. He had shifted the Ministry's official functions from those of inspection and control, to those of planning and service, giving this explanation to the Legislature in June 1968: "In all honesty, we must admit that while the tradition of a centralized system of education served the province well, it did lead to an undue emphasis on regimentation and conformity. This was perhaps a necessary evil in a pioneer society."

He proposed to diversify and decentralize the system. In fact his reforms imposed a new conformity and led to greater centralization.

How did it happen? Davis' omnibus bill was a mixed bag of educational reforms, some of them pedagogically good, others politically expedient. It was hard to sort out the difference. They all came in one package; each part seemed integral to the other. For example, it was obviously right to bring the elementary and secondary schools under one

[2] Laurence Iannacconne, professor at the University of California at Riverside, and one-time professor at OISE, told the May 1972 conference: "I know of nowhere else where a comparable reorganization of educational governance could have been achieved with as little dislocation. No state in the United States could have done it." *School Boards and the Political Fact,* Peter J. Cistone, editor, Ontario Institute for Studies in Education, 1972, p. 87.

board. This was portrayed as a reason for moving to county-sized districts, and while the two moves weren't interdependent, they were made to seem that way.

It was part of Davis' ingenuity to sell this new system as an essential part of a general reform movement. Amalgamation was made to seem the only feasible solution to inequity, and the hiring of large professional staffs came to be seen as the natural price of excellence.

Davis' initial actions put him on the map as an educational reformer, just as his later exploits as Premier made him Transit Man of the Year.[3] One admirer was Historian Fleming, who lauded Davis openly and warmly. But in the section on the aims of education, Fleming's comment turned ironic: "Davis has always been noted for his keen interest in various technological developments that promised to make education more efficient. He has found it necessary on occasion, however, to claim adherence to certain human values."

Some inkling into Davis' vision for the future is provided in a speech he gave at the Royal Bank of Canada's headquarters in May 1964. "Education: the Year 2064 as It Appears from 1964" was his title, and he envisioned the day when "each student must be taught . . . above all else, to communicate with computers, with his own and, through it, with those of others. . . . Our great-grandchildren, whether test tube or fullborn, will enter the 'school' of the future in the creche and nursery schools, being cared for by humans and robots but freeing the 'parents', from whom the genetic structure was fashioned, for work or recreation. Learning will begin at once, but imperceptibly so, as the proper environment is constructed and continuously altered to match growth and needs obtained by the genetic computer."

It is small comfort, perhaps, to be rescued from the

---

[3] He received the accolade from the American Transit Association at Miami Beach on October 15, 1973.

clutches of the classroom teacher by the talons of the machine, but as compensation Davis foresaw the benefits of individualized progress and one-to-one counselling. "The teacher would be consulted," he said, "when necessary, either face-to-face or by videophone, for direct instruction or explanation not available in programs or tapes." But the greatest innovations of all would come, Davis said, in "the administration, organization and supervision" of education, in which "relatively large and wealthy units or districts will be required." He would do his bit to bring the kingdom in.

Davis was borne to power by carrying out the priorities of his time, and the greatest priority from the standpoint of the central government was a more rational and adaptive system of control.

It is not a wholly one-sided picture. Davis did wipe out some of the more blatant vestiges of centralized control. He stopped the old inspectoral system that graded teachers and at times judged them harshly. He liquidated the grade 13 exams which had dominated the academic lives of 18-year-olds. He had the Grey Book, a 30-year-old guide to teachers of grades 1 to 6, superseded by new open-ended curriculum guides. And he liberalized the lock-step curriculum of secondary schools by instituting a credit system with free subject choices. In the age-old fight between Old Guard and progressives in the Ministry, he gave power to progressives such as Jack McCarthy and Kel Crossley, while also bringing technical advisors such as Tom Campbell into power.

These changes suited perfectly the euphoria of 1967, when petty grievances fell aside for Canada's centennial, when Flower Children made their one brief flourish, and Toronto trustees under William Ross' ebullient chairmanship, packed the senior high school population off to Montreal to attend Expo '67. The reforms were plums in the pudding, evidence that the freeing up of education was for real. Was it really? The proof was in the eating, and Davis' reformations had gone down whole.

What was happening was a basic shift in the method of control. Since the days of Ryerson, the province always held short rein over curriculum and teacher conduct. But it could not take over local school government. Ryerson never could force through his organizational schemes. Davis, quite the other way around, offered curricular and inspectoral autonomy, but he forced the school boards to amalgamate in such a way that both curriculum and inspection would come under bureaucratic control. The new larger school boards were expected to do for themselves what the province before had imposed upon them. By and large they accepted bureaucratic control and self-inspection after the provincial model as a feature of "equal educational opportunity." That was, after all, how the big city boards did it.

As it happened, Davis' move to consolidate school government eventually eclipsed his curricular reforms. The freeing up was largely illusionary. (The budget crackdown was soon to follow.) While it took away the constraints, it undercut the motive. Local initiative, the basis of true reform, was in short supply to create the sorts of changes the Ministry said it wanted.

Top-down reforms don't take very well. Ministerial officials are dimly aware of this. They see the fact that for innovations to stick, they have to be accepted by classroom teachers. They also suspect that it would be good if classroom teachers were collaborators in bringing about desired change. But they cannot accept the fact that reforms have to originate out there to be any good.

Top-down reforms put local schools through the pretense of adapting themselves to local needs, but it does not provide the breathing space for indigenous change. Those reforms have to fit the logic of the larger corporate system.

This twists the impetus toward relevance into bureaucratic molds, making it system-biased by forcing it through channels.

Three OISE professors commented in April 1973 that few of the innovations desired at the top had taken root in the schools. "This could be explained," they said, "by the fact that few changes have originated from within the school itself." They compared Ontario's system with that of England, and found Ontario's highly centralized, lacking the autonomy that made the English primary schools a success. Until Ontario allows local autonomy, they commented, "all liberal recommendations have a quality of unreality which can do little but produce cynicism and resistance among teachers."[4]

Even at the time, Davis' action wasn't without resistance. Ninety percent of the trustees answering a survey of the Ontario Public School Trustees' Association opposed the move. And from the town of Tavistock in Western Ontario came a message, dated Jan. 29, 1968. In an old-fashioned crackerbarrel style, it said amalgamation would hurt democracy and should not be imposed. Their response was transparently power-motivated and that, being local, was seen to be suspect. They seemed small-minded and reactionary. "Their traditional attitude had had a good deal to do with the government's resort to mandatory amalgamation," Fleming chided. Their vice was to be holdouts for a dying order of society, the self sufficient, rural and small town community that still believed it possible to work things out locally.

Local schooling seemed askew for no other reason that that it went against the then current dogma of progress. The

---

[4] Usha Ashlawat, J. Farrell, Vincent D'Oyley, "Administration as a Factor in the Implementation of Educational Innovations," *Comment on Education,* April 1973, pp. 20-25.

Hall-Dennis Report, *Living and Learning,* stated on page 12, flatly and without evidence: "But the small school and the local school board have outlived their day." And the Ontario Committee on Taxation reported in 1967 that provincial steps to eliminate rural school boards was itself "abundant testimony" to the fact that school units "can be too small to discharge their functions in an efficient and accountable manner."[5] Why such easy acceptance? The move toward amalgamation was trapped on the bandwagon of inevitability, the belief that what is happening all around is somehow self-validating.

Back of it were several major assumptions. One was that larger jurisdictions made good economic sense. Another was that equal educational opportunity was more possible in larger jurisdictions. A third was that, by some quirk of technology, larger jurisdictions gave more power to local communities.

None of these assumptions stand up to scrutiny. The economic rationale appeared to make the most sense of all. "Economy of scale has become an inescapable ingredient in the provision of education in Ontario," wrote David Cameron, a one-time Ministerial aide and subsequent defender of the county board system. He reasoned quite sensibly that special classes for the emotionally disturbed, retarded or perceptually handicapped could hardly be provided in a system so small it had only one or two children in each category. That logic seemed irrefutable if one accepted the categorization and segregation of children as the best way of teaching them. In fact, even the Ministry began to admit it was not the best way at about the time this massive reorganization came to pass.

But even accepting the argument as Cameron makes it, his assumptions are open to doubt. W.Z. Hirsch, a U.S.

[5] Volume 1, p. 57.

economist, analyzed the rising cost of education in 1959 and found many reasons to doubt the economies of large scale. "Large school districts . . ." he noted, "tend to lose efficiency because of political patronage and general administrative top-heaviness." Dr. James Coleman, at the end of a massive research program entitled *Equal Educational Opportunity*, concluded that he had discovered absolutely no evidence to indicate that costlier schools and costlier teaching equipment turned out better pupils. D.A. Dawson, an economics professor at McMaster University in Hamilton, did the only study every done on the economic benefits of large Ontario school districts. He weighed the costs per pupil against quality of education in 286 Ontario secondary school boards of all sizes. He found that "there would appear to be no clear-cut argument for consolidation of boards from an economies-of-scale point of view."

The second argument — that larger boards gave more power to school communities — was also open to question. For one thing, the larger districts made getting elected much more difficult that it had been in the small communities. It took money to run a successful campaign. This factor pushed the status of the elected elite higher on the socioeconomic spectrum. Peter Cistone discovered in his 1973 study of school trustees in Ontario that, whereas the median family income of the population was $7,880, the median school trustee earned — without his trustee honorarium — $14,340. Cistone stated flatly that they "are not representative of the population at large . . . school board members come disproportionately from the upper social-status groups."

Researcher Sondra Thorson did a study of York County attitudes in 1968, in which she found a sharp split between those who wanted centralization and those who did not:

Those trustees, officials, and teachers who favored the reorganization proposal were attuned to the scientific culture. By virtue of their education, occupation, age, relative mobility, their identification was with the scientific establishment, their orientation was universal, and they found an argument made in universal, scientific terms convincing.

Not so those who opposed the proposal. Their community was the local community, their values particularistic. An argument justified in terms of scientific reason was not convincing to them because their values and style of thought were not those of the scientific establishment. Their roots in their local communities were deep. Their education, occupation, age, stability, oriented them not to the scientific establishment but away from what they perceived a cold, impersonal bureaucracy of experts. What they sought was the warm, personal solidarity of the community.[6]

York County had an amalgamation proposal before it, and its council voted 19-6 against. Later, by Davis' general legislative decree, the county was forcibly amalgamated anyway. David Cameron notes in his own study of Ontario schools: "That the values underlying this reorganization are not shared by a significant portion of the population may well create serious consequences as the impact of the 1968 change becomes clearer."[7]

It seems hardly strange that the York Region, by all accounts Ontario's most progressive and efficient school district, suffered the province's longest teacher strike in early 1974. The surface issues were salaries and the right to negotiate working conditions, but underneath was a smoldering disenchantment with the management of this far-flung

---

[6] "Attitudes Towards School District Reorganization," an unpublished paper, the Ontario Institute for Studies in Education, 1968.
[7] *Schools for Ontario,* University of Toronto Press, 1972, page 230.

system. One of the strike's offshoots was a group of parents and students calling themselves WEB (Watching Education Bureaucracy), set up to combat what one founder called "the credibility gap between the board, the administration, the teachers and the community."[8]

An illustration of the changed climate comes from the old Orangeville Divisional Secondary District, where the whole school board once met on top of the Orangeville High School to inspect a roof that needed repair. They didn't do things like that once Dufferin County Board of Education took things over. They were able to afford a comptroller of plant, and they went inside to become the deliberative bodies within the bureaucracy.

Three years after consolidation, the high school teachers of Ontario did a rating of school boards. Their highest praise went to the Atikokan Board of Education, one of the very smallest by dint of its isolation in northern Ontario. I visited Atikokan, a coal mining town, in the spring of 1972 and found personal contact to be a strength the board had built on.

One of the three town doctors was the school board chairman; and prided himself in knowing the names of almost all the parents at the high school. I found it a tight-knit place, but at the same time progressive and open. "We kind of believe nobody is God Almighty in the system," said Kenneth Hay, the director of education, whose office was in the basement of an old public school. "And no one person should have the final authority in the system. Any student who's suspended can have a hearing if he appeals. The review group is a committee of the board and myself. This is threatening to the principal. It means that every decision he makes can be put on the line. But for that matter, every decision I make can be put on the line."

Teachers have a right of appeal, too, and Kenneth Hay

---

[8] *The Globe and Mail,* February 2, 1974.

feared constant polarization when they instituted that right. It never happened. "There's a kind of welding of the group together, and you can't really identify who's an administrator and who's a teacher". That's the director talking, of course, but it is note-worthy that Atikokan has a policy of teacher bonuses to boost their salaries to almost the level of principals, on the common sense theory that good teaching should be fully rewarded. "The greatest advantage we have is the size of the system," Donald Bailey, a young science teacher who moved up from St. Catharines, told me. "I have one person to go to, to get to the top man, and that's the director."

The whole secondary staff had a dance with the Board of Education once a year, and the 10-member board took a three-day planning conference with top staffers each year at Quetico Centre. It was far from an ideal system in many ways. John McTaggart, a Grade 11 student council member, had the usual complaints: "There's a lot of apathy in the school. Nobody but a few kids will do anything. . . . There are probably five teachers in the whole school that don't get shot down. . . ." But the system gained much from its small size that could not be measured in quantitative terms. It would be absurd to discount these benefits just because those in larger systems don't allow themselves to miss them.

Before long, the insulation became not merely size and distance, but bureaucracy itself. With their sharply upgraded tasks, trustees had no choice. Gradually, it became the administrators' job not just to run the program, but to enhance communication, to improve public relations, to create involvement. The wheel came full circle. The big boards ended up building a bureaucratic empire partly to counteract the effect of their own size. And the empire they created began to run by its own imperatives, which in turn conspired against person-to-person contact and open communication.

The shift to county boards was abetted by a widespread discrediting of political control. Power slipped willy-nilly from elected trustees to the highly paid professional, who was believed to be clean of politics and to do in a wholly disinterested fashion whatever it was that made kids learn.

The third argument — that of equal education opportunity — had on its side the simplistic logic of size. Some boards were large, some were small. The large ones could provide things the small ones couldn't, and vice versa. The solution was to make them all large. The assumptions were that the services of large boards were desirable, that the benefits of small boards were dispensable. "The main objective of the consolidation is to provide more equal opportunity in education," Davis said. "The plan creates units large enough to provide the special facilities now available in only the larger centres." That was *Globe and Mail* writer Terrance Wills' description of the change in 1968. Equal education, it now appears, was a code word for modelling the boards of the whole province after those of large cities.

The elaborate curricular and extra-curricular offerings of large city boards simply were not feasible in one-room or even ten-room operations. That much was clear. Little section schools were too small to provide the range of services — French teachers, diagnostic aides, classes for the retarded, subject consultants — the Ministry deemed necessary. It took a collection of size and numbers to accumulate the wherewithal of personnel and hardware. And these, in the Ministerial scheme of education, became the measures of equity.

The move to large jurisdictions promised many other benefits. It would integrate schooling for a child from kindergarten to grade 13. It would make all boards publicly elected and fiscally responsible. It would make the Ministry more capable of ironing out the fiscal differences among boards. Fleming lists all of these just as Davis gave them to the Legislature on March 14, 1968, adding his own comment: "In particular, Davis' interest in the use of expensive modern media such as educational television and his enthusiasm for the use of data processing techniques had implied the creation of administrative units of which the township areas could constitute only the first stage..."

From the Toronto experience he might have discovered, however, that the media could be available without being useful. The city's experience offers scant assurance that television, for example, could serve the schools as they are now organized. The Metro Educational Television Association polled area teachers in 1968 to find that few made use of television in the classroom. And in student services, Toronto likewise offers grave doubts. A graphic picture of how they fail comes from the Metropolitan Toronto Youth Services Study conducted by 12 young people during 1970. Chief researcher Robert Couchman found the schools "the largest, most expensive and unfortunately among the least effective" of all youth services in Metro. The annual report of one school social work department showed that each worker saw an average of three-quarters of a child per day over the entire school year.

To the Ministry, education is a service. As such it can be delivered much like welfare checks and dental care. The assumption was — and is — that it could be delivered better with standardized dispensary units. "In the past 10 years," said one Ministerial policy paper, "the (Ministry) has made significant strides in reordering the process of education delivery in Ontario, primarily through the establishment of large units of education administration and the delegation of increased responsibility to the school boards of these large units. This formation of larger units for education purposes was obviously required to eliminate the problems of organization and administration inherent in some varieties of

The Davis Imperative

school boards in Ontario at that time." Couched in suitable bureaucratese, it sounds convincing. The question it does not think to ask is whether the standardized fare is worth the delivery.

Education, for all its diverse nuances and unpredictability, had been reduced — organizationally, at least — to a model. The rational reasons behind the changes had to do with control more than learning, and this new structure allowed the province to enforce its dictates more readily.

Chapter 11

A LEARNING COMMUNITY

The bureaucracy of schooling creates people after its own image. Basic emotions and native gifts get turned inward and denied, while the outside stimuli to achieve, compete and conform become the driving force. When children learn at school to deny inner reality by accepting the outer imperatives, sociologists tell us — dispassionately — that this is socialization, which happens all the time, in any society. True, it does. But in our own situation we have to ask *what kind* of socialization it is, and whether we want it.

The school bureaucracy as it is serves the purposes of the province by serving its own needs. The ruling ethos of school government drives itself into the classroom by the implicit influences of bureaucratic control. Some have called this the hidden curriculum.

Certainly the liberal rhetoric of democracy has made little impact on schooling, as even its more clear-minded supporters will admit. As James Daly wrote in a candid defence of the system, "The term 'democracy' is a slogan that deceives and betrays. It gives nothing to the students but a sense of frustration because of its inherent impossibility." The system, rather, is built on obedience, loyalty and self-effacement and held together by a rigid network of power relationships. These are the home truths a child picks

A Learning Community

up in Grade 1, the message imprinted by the medium, whatever kind words disguise it. "At kindergarten," a Grade 1 child told me, "you just learn the rules. You learn not to stick your legs out when you sit on the floor, because they might trip someone, and things like that."

A child's first lesson is to accept the system's authority. After that, he can learn almost anything. This authority, as it relates to the classroom, is described so well in Judge R.W. Reville's prologue to his proposals on teacher salary negotiations: "The student comes, ignorant, in search of knowledge, and it is in the teacher's ability to communicate information to him that his power lies."[1]

It is a classic colonial power relationship, and here M. Mardjane in a fascinating footnote to *Learning to Be* makes the matter clear: "The colonial culture 'names' the world in its own way, substituting for the 'word' that colonized individual needs, in order to express his own world, the word which it uses as an instrument of domination."[2] Out of this authoritarian relationship the child is saddled with a cultural imperialism that denies his native feelings and strengths for the sake of survival at school.

Just as it subverts language, so it subverts a child's moral sense. Like Huck Finn, who knew he done wrong by helping Ole Jim escape slavery, the child finds himself in the grip of qualms that tell him his own good sense isn't right. The system's stamp of approval, the passing mark or simply the teacher's nod, more often than not negates the integrity of a growing child. It happens in the classroom because it happens all along the line. In the Board Chamber itself, the drama of individual powerlessness plays itself out, as trus-

---

[1] The report of the Committee of Inquiry into Negotiation Procedures, June 1972, the Ontario Legislature, page 4.

[2] "In most countries," Mardjane writes, "the school instead of being a centre for genuine dialogue — that is, an exchange of genuine words between teacher and learner in order to arrive at a still better understanding of the world — reflects colonial relationships." See *Learning to Be*, The Ontario Institute for Studies in Education, 1973, page 61.

tees vote resolutely for larger classes because the provincial or Metro authority says they must.

The end result is a creature of the system. The deeper feelings that do not count — hopelessness, anger, loneliness, love, solidarity and pride, to name a few — are covered over with a new range of adaptive behaviors.

These deep human drives, though suppressed, still express themselves in hurtful ways, and it is these expressions and the overlay of conformity that is then defined as the human condition, the model around which our schools are structured. The false front becomes the Good Life. Michael Maccoby the psychoanalyst, speaks of the human product as "the alienated centreless character" by which he refers to the kind of upbringing that ignores a child's contribution, forcing the child to disown his inner identity. Professor Irving Buchen observes much the same product but romanticizes it as "the collectivized individualist", and says the truly appropriate Twentieth Century man is one who incorporates outer forces into an amalgamated selfhood. Man is a part of all that he meets and nothing more.[3]

That isn't good enough. Some way or other we need to avoid the easy settlements, and the easiest one of all is to simply take the system as it comes. It is easy, in fact, to not even see it, because the machinations implanted in the brain so resemble the image of the machine.

But we begin to see.

We see that large classes, harried teachers, and tight timetables are essential to carrying out the real purposes of education.

We begin to see that an economy of emotional scarcity provides the setting in which human responses can be rationed, quantified and controlled.

We see that the new technologies often bring new con-

---

[3] "Humanism and Futurism: Enemies or Allies?" in *Learning for Tomorrow* edited by Alvin Toffler, Random House, 1974, pages 132 to 143.

trols in the very act of delivering us from the old.

We see that the ground rules of learning stem from the needs of the bureaucracy and the demands of the socio-economic system, more than from the needs of the learner.

We see that control has moved to the top, far removed from the true centre of growth and change, the person and the community.

We see how the school system tries to predict learning so as to encompass all eventualities and thus usurp the power of a learning community.

We see the folly of the neo-progressive goal of "warm, non-threatening, non-authoritarian relationships between teachers and learners" when the teachers themselves are subjected to harsh authoritarian demands.

Once we see where our jailed imaginations have kept us, there remains the struggle against the forces that keep us there. In the middle of that struggle we must also remove from our children the chains that have imprisoned us. While James Daly is correct in saying the school system is not democratic, the solution does not lie in assuming that democracy is an "inherent impossibility." We have to turn our minds towards just such possibilities, to try to discover a democratic process that will make sense of learning in the local community.

This takes going beyond Charles Silberman's liberal critique of schooling, *Crisis in the Classroom*, in which he lays out the realities in devastating detail, but then lays the fault to mere mindlessness. Those who "make a botch of it," he says, could mend their ways if they *thought* more about it. And it takes going beyond Herbert Gintis, a teacher at Harvard University, who finds Silberman's solution itself somewhat mindless. The faults of schooling, says Gintis, derive from the deep structures of society, they are no mere accidents of ignorance. For example, the teacher-as-boss syndrome is useful to those in power in an economy where workers have no control over personal or group activities in factory, office and community.

The schools in Canada are part of the larger logic of a political economy that sanctions the conditioning of students to its uses, however harmful that process is to them. Certain oppressed groups in society — among the working and welfare poor, the teachers, the Indians, the artist communities — are fighting back against that larger logic. But the fight needs to be not just the unionist's battle for better wages and working conditions; it must wrestle too with the inward emptiness of human life and the shattered sense of community. The socialist critique offers a fair assessment of social reality, a good basis for outward political struggle. But it too often neglects the psycho-social underpinnings of oppression. The struggle is deeply personal as well as boldly political. Unless we somehow contend with what Wilhelm Reich described as "the emotional plague" we will hardly be able to rearrange society to liberate ourselves.[4]

The schools do not have to be the agents of a centralized bureaucracy. That bureaucracy has been the crucible for the founding of an industrial state, but no longer can it cling to the myth of inevitability that held it in place. We know now that its routines and disciplines distort the learning process for alien political ends, that the postulate of Alfred Whitehead in *The Aims of Education* some 45 years ago has reached fruition. The key fact of education, he said, is that "necessary technical excellence can only be acquired by training which is apt to damage those energies of mind which

---

[4] Reich describes in *Character Analysis* how the neurosis passes from generation to generation. Without deliberate intent, despite the best of precautions, adults pass on to their children their own conflicts, in whatever inverted or twisted forms, so that each generation becomes as neurotically burdened as the one before. "We cannot believe in a satisfactory human existence," Reich wrote, "as long as biology, psychiatry and pedagogy do not come to grips with the universal emotional plague and fight it as ruthlessly as one fights plague-transmitting rats." Page 280.

should direct the technical skill." George Grant of McMaster University restated the quandary in *Technology and Empire*. The same cultural chemistry that makes us leaders in technique, he said, "stands as a barrier to any thinking which might be able to comprehend technique from beyond its own dynamism." There has to be another way to do it.

The kind of schooling I envision would have to start with "the human being in community". It would have to find a centre, some base of strength and integrity attuned to the primary human needs and the essential community functions. Each small unit, forming a part of the larger political struggle, would need to be local, democratic, regenerative and integrative. I will explain what I mean by those words in the next few pages, but first to set out clearly the kind of school government I have in mind.[5]

It would entail, quite simply, a local council at each school made up of teachers, parents, local residents and older students. This could come through the evolution of the advisory school councils to positions of decision-making power. The council would appoint staff members, decide the curriculum, establish the school discipline, and disperse operating funds. The overall Board of Education would have a strictly limited role: it would apportion funds equitably among schools, negotiate staff salaries, and serve as a tribunal for disputes between councils or among individuals. The principal at each school would serve as the executive of each council. This would entail a drastic but orderly dispersal of power to local communities that sought it, and a carefully staged dismantling of the bureaucratic empire.

To do this means to push beyond conventional limits, such as those laid out by Ed Stewart while deputy minister of education. He declared debates having to do with local-versus-central-authority to be "non-constructive in their na-

[5] I have spelled it out in greater detail in *Must Schools Fail? The Growing Debate in Canadian Education*, edited by Niall Byrne and Jack Quarter, McClelland and Stewart Ltd., 1972, pages 162 to 174.

ture" and therefore beyond the realm of useful discourse.[6] But of course, at the summit of power, such questions look silly. Yet in reality, to avoid them is to indulge in the shallowest forms of educational debate, the kind that can only keep public education confined to existing quarters.

Local. The schools need to become aware of their geography and neighborhood. Ecology itself seems to point us in the direction of re-valuing the land, the air, the water, the environment we use every day. Ecology has global dimensions, it is true, but I don't know if we can conserve the planet until we regain the ground beneath our feet. Yet a still stronger motive for local community is the necessity to create enclaves of stability and power as counterbalance to a swiftly changing technocratic order. It is fashionable to argue against neighborhoods on grounds that modern transit and communications have made them anachronistic. The contemporary thing has become the "community of mutual interest," which transcends local boundaries. But to ignore neighborhood is to give up the most natural and stable chance for democratic schooling. This is the old idea that the learning community needs to be the living community to avoid alienation and splitting off. To shut ourselves off from community is to neglect a large part of ourselves, and to regain it will reveal new strengths.

Local communities have emerged in the past decade as centres of civic concern and renewal. As Albert Rose says in *Governing Metropolitan Toronto*, they had almost no impact on civic government before 1965, but by 1972 they had helped throw out a pro-development City Council and had started a major swing toward ecological care and neighborhood preservation. This action came out of struggles in middle and working class communities, out of the fight in the

---

[6] Change and the Public Attitude Toward Education, by Ed Stewart, *Ontario Education,* January/February 1973, page 5.

A Learning Community

Annex against the Spadina Expressway, in the Kensington area against bulldozer urban renewal, and in Trefann Court for the right of local communities to direct their own redevelopment. The very strength of those movements shows Toronto to be one place on the continent where local community survives. Representative democracy has served us poorly in this regard, but it has not damaged the local entity beyond repair.

But public education remains aloof. It is still considered too delicate a matter to be exposed to political influence, and in that regard we have been brainwashed. In fact, it is too delicate a matter to be left to centralized control. The reason it remains there is that we have not the mind to admit how destructive that is nor the will to free it.

The system's own school experiments — such as project SEED, the non-structured high school, and Alpha, the parent-directed open school for primary children — have by and large ignored neighborhood. Alpha, run by middle-class academic parents, took up space at the Broadview YMCA in a community where few of them lived. Project SEED drew mainly from North Toronto's upper-middle-class, taking space in the YMHA at Bloor Street and Spadina Avenue. Both schools were safety valves in the mechanics of schooling, drawing away from local schools the parental impact that might have transformed them into more democratic places.

Democratic. To establish democracy in schooling usually looks like anarchy to those in control. Their own life style and social status depend on the system staying put. This sometimes accounts for nervous over-reactions. The Park School crash reading program was one knee-jerk attempt to compensate for past neglect. The proposed Task Force on Education during 1971-73 also had the qualities of a bush-fire squad, quelling inner-city angers to ameliorate the larger school structure. This syndrome also partly accounts for the drive to set up "community schools" to offer full services without decision-making power.

The bureaucracy tries to respond to community wants even before being set to it by the trustees, to ensure contentment and maintain its credibility. But rather than share decision-making power, educators hide behind the ruse that parents could bring in the hickory stick or destroy the progressive methods they have perfected at school. Involvement, though, would mollify the rigid views of many parents who now watch the school uneasily from a distance, and just possibly reveal a less reactionary mind-set than teachers, from their distance, had feared.

There have been some movements toward involvement in local school communities as well, on a sporadic, ad hoc basis. Local communities with the aid of a reform-minded Board in 1970 put a timely end to the expansionary practices of Comptroller of Buildings Harry Facey. In Kensington, the community saved nine houses and then took a hand in planning the Kensington Community School. And at Brown Public School near St. Clair Avenue, the community won an immersion French program over administrative opposition, and also took part in the planning of a new building.

Upper-middle class communities have always held formidable — but informal — power over local schooling through such groups as the Home and School Associations, especially in North Toronto. There are few groups like that in working-class, inner-city schools, yet two thirds of the Toronto public school population is working class. In fact, 43 per cent occupies the lowest socio-economic category in Professor Bernard Blishen's index of occupations.[7] The lack of organized citizen groups in working-class communities

---

[7] See Edgar Wright, Student's Background and its Relationship to Class and Programme in School (The Every Student Survey), Research Department, Toronto Board of Education, December 1970, page 18.

leaves the education of the poor almost totally in the hands of middle-class educators. The hardiest exception in recent years was the Park School Council, which had some impact on reading and special education during the early 1970's. Another recent hope is the renascent ethnic grouping, such as the Chinese and Greek Parents Associations. The attempts at parental involvement so far have been fearful and sporadic in the inner city.

But not just administrators fear local democracy. Parents fear it too. Administrators fear to lose power, parents fear to lose powerlessness, an equally frightening prospect. Even where inferior education has driven parents to despair, they shy away. The institutions seem too forbidding, the odds appear too great, the personal sense of power too small. And to get involved in school means confronting one's own anguish around schooling, which few of us are able to do for very long without personal crisis.

But unless democracy comes to schooling, there is little point in teaching it at school. Pupils can memorize the forms of parliamentary procedure and study the great ideals, but the double message will continue turning them into sentimentalists or cynics. I am not suggesting that young children be equal partners, but that parents and teachers be involved together in their interest, which means the young must be carefully heard.

A teacher who is no longer powerless in the community of adults will have less psychological need to lord it over the pupils. It is axiomatic that a person teaches what a person learns, and to break through into a truly liberating learning situation entails new ventures of this sort. Furthermore, I don't know of any better way to overcome the mistrust between parents and teachers than to hassle it out in a responsible, democratic forum.

Regenerative. In some way the healing of fractured lives

needs to go on at the basic level of personality. When this occurs people will be able to get in touch with their instincts, talents and strengths. Under bureaucratic auspices, though, it hasn't worked. Too much is invested in papering over the inner conflicts with outer proprieties, as symbolized in the old title for the system's psychological department, Child Adjustment Services.

But it won't do to simply cut loose from the bureaucracy. The parents and teachers who started the Alpha Experiment in 1972 were all but swamped with personality conflicts in the first four months. Roger Simon, a teacher at the Ontario Institute for Studies in Education and one of the parents involved, told me later, "There's no way the problems of Alpha in its first year can be laid to the system. I really believe that we were just inept. The big difference is that although an ordinary school is inept as well, the ineptitude there is hidden, and it was all out in the open at Alpha." He had envisioned Alpha as a "psychological-social community" but it never happened that way in the trauma of starting out with 100 children in barely finished quarters at the old Broadview Y.

Looking back later, Simon and colleague Malcolm Levin wrote about the need for an adult core group, a source of acceptance and strength against feelings of isolation, frustration and powerlessness. They found many innovators unready to learn from others.[8] But this unreadiness derives I think from the fact that most school reforms settle for the same neurotic base that sustains the old system, which is not deep enough to make the vital difference.

The common, alienating neurosis can become comfortable even if it demeans human life, deadens the potential for growth, and does injury to the young. We begin with the

[8] "The Creation of Education Settings: A Developmental Perspective," by Malcolm Levin and Roger Simon, Ontario Institute for Studies in Education, July 1973.

awareness that the problem of powerlessness is personal, too. As one stirs the possibility of power, one clashes with that thorn hedge of defenses built against one's own freedom, but there has to be a place to make that struggle.

Toronto's Counterfoil Group, an association of ten persons trying to redefine the nature of public education, dealt with this problem by proposing "anti-psychologists". These would be people who — instead of working out technologies of anxiety reduction — would try to bring people together for, as they put it, "self-revelation and interpretation of collective reality."[9] They would work for and with community groupings. This is something quite different from serving as a lubricant to the system by helping people cope with the anxiety caused by alienation and competition. Of course, a psychologist who helps people gain a sense of their own strengths and a critical awareness of the power structures is not going to be paid for it very long by the school system. This sort of thing will begin and end in the local community, but its repercussions could be great.

To adopt this approach along with structural reform entails an awareness that restructuring alone won't work. Providing a local democratic setting for learning will remove many obstacles, but its potential can always be undercut if the internal struggle is neglected.

Integrative. The scourge of streaming has to end. It is one practice that more than any other spells trouble in the system, yet it is as old as the Toronto system itself, and an integral part of it. Through streaming the schools retain the dominance of the middle class at the expense of those at the bottom, promoting students on an apparently equitable basis that remains harshly discriminatory. It is not good enough, for it fosters a smug elitism that maintains the gross dis-

---

[9] "One Alternative to Technocracy," in *The City: Attacking Modern Myths*, edited by Alan Powell, McClelland and Stewart Ltd., page 239.

parities of Canadian society. To change this, at this late date, requires a very radical beginning.

The problem is not that individual differences are paid too much attention — they are not paid enough. The problem lies with the criteria of competition. Learning persons should be free to explore to a point where the norm loses its meaning; each individual should be encouraged to stand by his personal and communal experience.

And certainly social class conflict will surface at the local level, just as now it moulders throughout the entire system. But perhaps then it can at least be seen and confronted for what it is. Again it is no foregone conclusion that local democratic government in itself will take schools off the competitive treadmill. But then at least a community awareness might evolve to give new variations to the process of learning, and make communities rather than individuals the locus of success.

A change of awareness demands a new order, and the model most likely to bring it is the local community in all its permutations. It is here that struggling people may best extend themselves into political beings, and they do so best by the very act of extending community. Local democracy has never been overly popular anywhere for long. As Hannah Arendt points out in *On Revolution,* local councils swiftly devolve into centralized forms of control. " . . . They failed to understand," she writes of the early statesmen of the Western democracies, "to what an extent the council system confronted them with an entirely new form of government, with a new public space for freedom . . ." What happened instead was that centralized state authorities usurped the authority of local bodies, then delegated limited functions back to the local communities. It was a top-down flow of authority; the natural course of democratic government had been overturned. It is time in the Canadian experience, within its tradition of conservative reform, to restore the powers of the local community.